The Complete Plant-Based Diet for Beginners
© Copyright 2023 by Harber Curry

This document is geared towards providing exact and reliable information with regards to the topic and issue covered. The publication is sold with the idea that the publisher is not required to render accounting, officially permitted, or otherwise, qualified services. If advice is necessary, legal or professional, a practiced individual in the profession should be ordered.

From a Declaration of Principles which was accepted and approved equally by a Committee of the American Bar Association and a Committee of Publishers and Associations.

In no way is it legal to reproduce, duplicate, or transmit any part of this document in either electronic means or in printed format. Recording of this publication is strictly prohibited and any storage of this document is not allowed unless with written permission from the publisher.

All rights reserved.

The information provided herein is stated to be truthful and consistent, in that any liability, in terms of inattention or otherwise, by any usage or abuse of any policies, processes, or directions contained within is the solitary and utter responsibility of the recipient reader. Under no circumstances will any legal responsibility or blame be held against the publisher for any reparation, damages, or monetary loss due to the information herein, either directly or indirectly.

Respective authors own all copyrights not held by the publisher.

The information herein is offered for informational purposes solely, and is universal as so.

The presentation of the information is without contract or any type of guarantee assurance.

The trademarks that are used are without any consent, and the publication of the trademark is without permission or backing by the trademark owner.

All trademarks and brands within this book are for clarifying purposes only and are the owned by the owners themselves, not affiliated with this document.

Copyright © 2023 by Harber Curry
All rights reserved. No part of this book may be reproduced, scanned, or distributed in any printed or electronic form without permission.

First Edition: November 2023

Cover: Illustration made by French B.

Printed in the United States of America

TABLE OF CONTENTS

INTRODUCTION .... Page 1

CHAPTER 1 -
    BENEFITS OF A PLANT-BASED DIET... « 3

CHAPTER 2 -
    PLANT-BASED NUTRITION BASICS.. « 13

CHAPTER 3 -
    STOCKING A PLANT-BASED PANTRY... « 23

CHAPTER 4 -
    ENERGIZING BREAKFASTS.. « 35

CHAPTER 5 -
    SATISFYING LUNCHES... « 45

CHAPTER 6 -
    NOURISHING DINNERS.. « 55

CHAPTER 7 -
    SAVORY SNACKS AND APPETIZERS... « 65

CHAPTER 8 -
    DELECTABLE DESSERTS.. « 75

BONUS 1 -
    AUDIOBOOK... « 85

BONUS 2 -
    14 TUTORIALS FOR BEGINNERS.. « 87

BONUS 3 -
    47 ADVANCED TUTORIALS... « 89

BONUS 4 -
    BASIC EVERYONE SHOULD KNOW...................................... « 91

EXCLUSIVE BONUS -
    3 EBOOK.. « 93

AUTHOR BIO -
    HARBER CURRY.. « 95

Dedicated to all my friends and to all the people
who gave me their help.
Thanks a lot
Thanks to all of you for your confidence
in my qualities and what I do.
Harber Curry

INTRODUCTION

For many people, the choice to adopt a plant-based diet stems from a desire to live a healthier, more ethically conscious, and environmentally sustainable lifestyle. Numerous scientific studies have shown that reducing or eliminating animal products and emphasizing whole, minimally processed plant foods instead can offer noteworthy advantages for human health. From lowering heart disease risk factors to supporting a healthy body weight, the perks of plant-based eating are far-reaching.

Shifting away from meat and dairy in favor of more veggies, fruits, whole grains, beans, lentils, nuts and seeds has been associated with improved cardiovascular health outcomes. In a major 2013 meta-analysis involving over 250,000 participants, vegetarian diets were linked with significantly lower blood pressure and cholesterol levels compared to non-vegetarian diets. The vegetarians also benefited from a 29% reduction in mortality from heart disease. These protective effects are likely due to the cholesterol-free nature of plant foods, as well as their abundance of antioxidants and anti-inflammatory phytochemicals. Fiber-rich plant foods also promote lower cholesterol by binding to bile acids in the digestive tract.

In addition to enhancing heart health, plant-based diets are conducive to achieving and maintaining a healthy body weight. Multiple studies indicate that vegetarians and vegans tend to have lower BMI compared to their meat-eating counterparts. For example, in the Adventist Health Study-2 involving over 60,000 participants, vegans had the lowest mean BMI. Plant foods are naturally low in calories while being high in water and fiber - a combination that helps you feel satiated on fewer calories. Fiber slows digestion, regulating blood sugar response. This satiating quality allows a plant-based style of eating to be an effective tool for managing weight goals.

Further evidence indicates additional advantages such as lower blood pressure, reduced type 2 diabetes risk, and lower cancer rates in those following predominately plant-based diets. The lower risks are partially attributed to more optimal body weight as well as the protective components within plant foods themselves. Antioxidants including vitamin C, vitamin E and polyphenols fight free radical damage that can lead to chronic disease. Plants also contain an array of anti-inflammatory phytochemicals which can help regulate the inflammatory response underlying many illnesses.

Beyond personal health, adopting plant-based eating habits supports the greater planetary health and helps preserve resources for future generations. Animal agriculture remains a major contributor to environmental degradation, emitting substantial greenhouse gases as well as requiring land, water and fossil fuels. Based on Life Cycle Assessments, plant-based foods have a much lower environmental impact overall, generating far fewer GHG emissions while using less water and cropland compared to most animal products.

Last but not least, eliminating animal products aligns with ethical motivations to avoid subsidizing factory farm systems that deprive animals of natural freedoms and comforts. Rather than commodifying sentient beings, plant-based eaters opt for more compassionate nourishment. Although following a strict plant-based diet is not feasible or appropriate for every individual, simply reducing intake of animal products does make a meaningful difference. Every plant-based meal enjoyed lessens your personal carbon footprint while withdrawing financial support for undesirable industrial farming practices.

CHAPTER 1

BENEFITS OF A PLANT-BASED DIET

Improved health

One of the most compelling reasons people choose to go plant-based is to improve their overall health and reduce their risk of chronic diseases. A wealth of research has demonstrated the protective effects of vegetarian and vegan diets against numerous conditions that are devastatingly common in the Western world.

By focusing your diet on whole, minimally processed plant foods instead of animal products, you empower your body with antioxidants, fiber, beneficial plant compounds, and nutrients that optimize health. Plants contain no cholesterol and little saturated fat, both of which are heavily implicated in heart disease. Fiber fills you up, improves digestion and gut microbiome balance, and supports weight management. Phytochemicals found exclusively in the plant kingdom provide antioxidant, anti-inflammatory, and anticancer activity.

A plant-based diet has been shown to lower cholesterol, blood pressure, inflammation, insulin resistance, and other risk factors for cardiovascular disease. The Adventist Health Studies found that vegetarians have a lower incidence of heart disease, diabetes, and hypertension compared to meat-eaters. Plant-based diets reduce visceral fat stores around organs, which drives metabolic dysfunction. The fiber, potassium, magnesium, and vitamin C in plant foods improve blood flow, artery flexibility, and oxygen delivery to cells.

Cruciferous vegetables, berries, whole grains, nuts, and tea contain flavonoids that enhance blood vessel function. Greens, sweet potatoes, avocado, tomatoes, and carrots provide carotenoids that protect against atherosclerosis. Plant sterols in nuts, seeds, whole grains, and produce have cholesterol-lowering effects. Garlic, onions, herbs and spices confer cardioprotective benefits. Meat, dairy, and eggs contain none of these protective components.

Cancer is similarly impacted by diet and lifestyle factors. Links have been made between diets high in red and processed meats and colorectal cancer risk. Plants contain a huge diversity of anticancer phytochemicals that offer multifactorial protection: antioxidants ward off DNA damage, anti-inflammatories suppress cancer promotion, and anti-angiogenics inhibit tumor growth by blocking blood vessel formation.

Cruciferous vegetables exhibit anticancer activity, particularly against hormone-related cancers. Berries, green tea, and soy foods have also demonstrated cancer-fighting abilities. Fiber speeds waste transit time, binding and diluting potential carcinogens. Obesity drives cancer progression, making plant-based diets' role in weight management helpful for prevention.

Type 2 diabetes used to be called adult-onset diabetes, but over the past 30 years, cases have skyrocketed in youth. The best strategy to avoid becoming one of the 100 million American adults with diabetes or prediabetes is through diet and activity patterns. Plant-based diets rich in high-fiber foods with a low glycemic load help regulate blood sugar and insulin sensitivity.

Multiple studies have shown that vegetarian and vegan diets improve glycemic control and decrease medication needs in diabetics better than conventional diabetic diets. Plant foods do not spike blood sugar as drastically as refined carbs and sweets. Fiber slows carbohydrate absorption and reduces insulin secretion. Healthy fats and proteins buffer glycemic response when eaten with carbs. Antioxidants reduce oxidative stress that contributes to impaired insulin signaling. Going plant-based helps maintain a healthy weight since plants are low in calories yet high in nutrients that satiate. Obesity is the number one predictor of type 2 diabetes.

Plant-based diets may also offer protective effects against chronic conditions like Alzheimer's and Parkinson's diseases. These both involve oxidative damage, inflammation, and protein aggregation in the brain. The antioxidants and phytochemicals in fruits, vegetables, spices, coffee, and tea help mitigate these degenerative processes. B vitamins like folate and B6 support neurological health, with deficiency linked to cognitive decline. Beans and lentils provide iron to prevent anemia and oxygenate the brain.

The nutrition and lifestyle factors within a plant-based framework combine to make it a powerful approach for achieving optimal wellness and longevity. While no diet guarantees perfect health, by filling your plate with whole plant foods instead of animal products, you set yourself on the right track for reducing risk and promoting protective aspects that ward off chronic diseases. Banana

Weight management

For many, a central motivation for adopting a plant-based diet is to better manage body weight and avoid obesity. Rates of overweight and obesity are high worldwide, with 39% of adults being overweight and 13% being obese globally in 2016. Excess body weight significantly raises disease risks including heart disease, stroke, type 2 diabetes, and certain cancers. Thankfully, a whole food plant-based diet can be an effective tool for achieving long-term weight loss and maintenance.

Multiple observational studies tracking BMI in vegetarians and vegans have found lower mean body weights compared to non-vegetarians. For instance, within the Adventist Health Study-2 cohort, vegans had the lowest mean BMI of 23.6 kg/m2 whereas non-vegetarians had a mean BMI of 28.8 kg/m2. This association suggests plant-based diets are conducive to optimal weight status. Clinical trials of plant-based diets for weight loss also reveal promising results. In a recent 2021 study, overweight adults following a low-fat vegan diet for 16 weeks lost an average of 13 pounds compared to no weight change for the control group.

Plant foods power weight loss via several mechanisms. First, plants are naturally low in calories yet high in beneficial fiber and water content. For the same volume of food, salad greens, broth-based soups, and blended smoothies provide far fewer calories than high-fat meat or cheese-based dishes. Consuming fiber-rich whole plant foods helps regulate appetite by slowing digestion, increasing satiety, and stabilizing blood sugar response. This allows you to feel satisfied on fewer calories, making plant foods ideal for weight management.

Calorie density is another distinct advantage. Beans, lentils, starchy vegetables, fruits and whole grains deliver a larger volume of food per calorie compared to oils, processed carbs, and animal products. You can eat a greater quantity of food while keeping calories in check. For instance, 500 calories of cooked grains and beans offers far more nutrients and satisfaction than 500 calories of oils, butter, cheese or meat.

Additionally, plant foods boost metabolism via their thermogenic effect. Your body expends extra calories breaking down fiber and metabolizing plant protein. Certain compounds like capsaicin from chilies and EGCG from green tea also provide a mild metabolic boost. Together, these factors make plant foods uniquely helpful for achieving calorie deficits needed for weight loss.

To leverage the weight loss potential of plant-based eating, meal plans should emphasize minimally processed whole foods. Focus on plentiful vegetables, fruits, whole grains, legumes, nuts and seeds. Limit oils, refined flours, sugars and mock meats which are higher in calories. Enjoy an array of satisfying whole food plant proteins like lentils, beans, tofu, tempeh, seitan and edamame. Stay well hydrated with water, herbal tea, or vegetable broth. Portion control remains key for weight loss, so use mindful eating practices.

A whole food plant-based pattern removes the common pitfalls that undermine weight management attempts. Often excess calories, fat, sodium and sugar from processed and animal-based foods sabotage efforts. The innate properties of fiber-rich minimally processed plant foods boost satiation on fewer calories, facilitating sustainable weight loss. Other lifestyle factors like adequate sleep, stress management and regular activity further complement your plant-based diet.

For lasting results, transition to plant-based eating as a lifestyle, rather than a temporary fix. Make gradual changes, focusing on crowding out overly processed foods with more whole plant options. Consider enlisting social support through plant-based groups. Track your progress with before/after photos or other metrics besides the scale. Celebrate non-scale victories like boosted energy, clearer skin or better digestion. The journey to your healthiest weight consists of many small, positive steps. A whole food plant-based pattern provides the optimal framework.

Lower environmental impact

Adopting a plant-based diet is one of the most effective ways for an individual to reduce their carbon footprint and minimize environmental harm. Animal agriculture places an immense strain on natural resources and directly contributes to issues like climate change, pollution, deforestation, and species extinction. By choosing plant foods over meat and dairy, anyone can slash their eco-impact and be part of creating a sustainable future.

To understand how impactful dietary changes can be, it helps to grasp the full extent of the environmental issues caused by modern industrial animal agriculture. The clearing of forests to graze livestock and grow feed crops is a huge driver of deforestation, destroying vital wildlife habitats and releasing stored carbon. Animal waste and fertilizers pollute waterways and oceans, causing algal blooms that deplete aquatic life.

Additionally, ruminant livestock like cows and sheep generate methane, an extremely potent greenhouse gas that traps heat in the atmosphere. Agriculture alone accounts for around 15% of global greenhouse gas emissions, with animal-based foods much more GHG-intensive than plant crops. By shifting demand away from these products, plant-based diets significantly mitigate food-related climate change impacts.

The resources needed to produce meat, dairy and eggs also far exceed what is required for most plant foods. Beef has a staggering water footprint of approximately 1,800 gallons per pound. That means just one hamburger patty requires over 900 gallons of water to produce! The water demand for plant-based staples like beans, grains and vegetables is dramatically lower across the board. With many regions facing severe water shortages, dietary changes can help relieve the strain.

Raising livestock is also an inefficient use of arable land that could otherwise be used to grow food directly for human consumption. For the amount of crops like corn and soy fed to US livestock, we could feed about 800 million people instead. With global hunger still a critical issue, shifting toward plant-based diets allows us to allocate resources where they are needed most.

These are just some examples of how excessive consumption of animal foods damages the environment and diverts limited resources. Fortunately, transitioning to a predominantly plant-based diet can substantially mitigate a person's negative impact. Replacing meat and dairy with fruits, vegetables, grains, beans, lentils, nuts and seeds is consistently shown to shrink dietary carbon and water footprints.

In fact, one study found that going fully vegan could reduce an individual's carbon footprint by up to 73%. Plant-based diets also use far less land and release much lower amounts of GHG emissions and waste into the ecosystem. Promoting more sustainable plant-centric diets is now a focus of major environmental organizations like the UN and World Wildlife Fund.

While dietary shifts are critical, environmental benefits also depend on how plants are produced. Choosing organic produce, supporting regenerative agriculture methods and reducing food waste are key ways to further minimize impacts. Locally grown foods also help by reducing transport emissions. Luckily, plant-based options provide flexibility to source whole foods in the most eco-friendly ways.

Transitioning to plant-based eating allows people to take a stand against the major environmental destruction wrought by modern animal agriculture. While systemic changes to how food is produced are still needed, consumer choices can help drive companies and governments to enact more sustainable practices. Through individual dietary change and advocacy, a plant-powered future is possible.

Making greener choices has never been easier thanks to the growing selection of plant-based products on shelves and restaurant menus. And as more people join the movement, plant-based living will become even more accessible, affordable and mainstream. By using your dollars to support companies with eco-conscious principles, you empower them to keep expanding.

While the plant-based journey does require some adjustments, it is one of the most profound ways for individuals to lessen their personal environmental impact. The recipes and tips in this book will show you how satisfying and attainable plant-based eating can be. Your choice to help the planet by putting plants on your plate will also benefit your health, community and personal values.

Animal welfare

Choosing plant-based foods over animal products is one of the most powerful ways we can take a stand against cruelty to animals. By withdrawing support for industries that exploit animals for food, clothing, research and entertainment, we decrease demand and production. Going plant-based helps end immense suffering experienced by billions of animals each year in factory farming.

The scale of animal agriculture is staggering - over 9 billion livestock animals are raised and killed annually in the US alone. Chickens, pigs, cows and other animals suffer immensely on industrial farms in extreme confinement, deprived of natural behaviors, pumped with hormones and antibiotics, subjected to painful procedures, and killed once productivity wanes.

99% of farm animals in the US come from factory farms. Images and videos from undercover investigations at these facilities have exposed horrific conditions - sick or injured animals left to suffer, mother pigs unable to turn around in gestation crates, chickens bred to grow so fast their legs break under their own weight. These industries treat living beings like raw materials and production units rather than sentient creatures deserving of a decent life.

By choosing plant milks, meats, cheeses and eggs, we opt out of supporting these cruel systems. Our purchases drive production - what we demand, companies will supply. Consumer rejection of animal products is disrupting major food corporations, forcing them to introduce plant-based product lines as the market grows. This represents meaningful change.

Going plant-based also spares animals used for apparel and accessories. Purchasing vegan clothing and shoes made from innovative plant and synthetic materials instead of leather, fur, wool and down prevents substantial animal exploitation. 400 million animals are killed for fur alone each year. Sheep raised for wool production often endure mulesing. Down feathers come from birds living in torturous conditions.

Vegan clothing options have never been more abundant and stylish. Premium brands like Matt & Nat, Native Shoes, and Save The Duck offer high-quality animal-free fashion and footwear. Fast fashion retailers like H&M are expanding vegan collections in response to increasing consumer demand. Consumer dollars steer the market and company practices.

In addition to farmed animals, adopting a plant-based lifestyle helps end demand for captive wildlife entertainment. Animals like dolphins, elephants, tigers and monkeys suffer tremendously in circuses, theme parks and illegal exotic pet trade. Going to performances involving captive wildlife supports these harmful practices. A plant-based lifestyle means avoiding such exploitation for entertainment.

Perhaps most difficult is the question of animal testing and vivisection. Seeking out cruelty-free cosmetics, household products and medicines that were not tested on animals is an important commitment. However, most pharmaceutical drugs and medical devices use animal trials during R&D. This complex issue lacks easy individual solutions, but social and institutional change can end reliance on animal models in favor of advanced human tissue research methods.

Taking an animal rights stance goes beyond just diet to carefully examining how our choices may economically support systemic abuse and exploitation. From fashion to entertainment to research, moving toward plant-based and cruelty-free options helps enact social change. Our collective shift to plant foods will continue disrupting and dismantling the animal industrial complex.

Reducing and eliminating animal product demand makes a monumental difference. Hundreds of millions of animals are now spared the misery of industrial farming due to the expanding plant-based movement. That number will keep rising as more people join in. We have the power to withdraw financial support from destructive systems and stop our complicity in violence against animals.

Walking the talk with our purchases is vital, but speaking up is also essential for creating change. We can contact companies to request more plant-based and compassionate options. We can expose animal cruelty through social media. We can lobby government representatives to pass animal welfare legislation. We can support farm animal sanctuaries financially and by volunteering or visiting. There are countless ways to create kinder systems.

At the deepest level, choosing a plant-based lifestyle manifests the principles of non-violence and doing no harm. This honors the interconnectedness of all life. Making compassionate choices allows us to align our actions with our ethics. From an environmental standpoint, animal agriculture wastes resources and pollutes the earth. But the fundamental reason for rejecting animal exploitation is that caring for animals is simply the right thing to do. The plant-based movement offers hope for a world with less suffering.

Harber Curry

CHAPTER 2
PLANT-BASED NUTRITION BASICS

Protein

Protein is an essential macronutrient that serves vital functions in building, repairing, and maintaining tissues and cells throughout the body. Unlike the fat and carbohydrates, protein cannot be stored, so we require a regular dietary supply. Animal products like meat, eggs, and dairy are packed with protein, so it's understandable that the nutrient can seem challenging to get on a plant-based diet. However, with a small amount of planning and knowledge, getting sufficient daily protein is simple.

All whole plant foods contain at least some protein. Certain plant foods are especially high in protein - beans, lentils, peas, nuts, seeds, soy foods, and even green vegetables have substantial amounts. As long as calories are adequate, it is nearly impossible to develop a protein deficiency on a varied plant-based diet. Research shows that vegetarians and vegans generally meet or exceed recommended protein intakes when total caloric intake is sufficient.

Combining different plant proteins within a meal or throughout the day results in a complete amino acid profile. Beans and rice, peanut butter sandwiches, tofu scrambles with veggies, and trail mixes marrying nuts and seeds are all examples of plant-based protein pairings. No need to meticulously combine proteins at each meal - your body pools amino acids over the course of a day.

Varying protein sources from meal to meal and day to day easily provides all essential amino acids. As long as you regularly eat beans, grains, nuts and seeds, you will meet protein requirements on a plant-based diet. No need to track or tally protein grams.

Some of the most protein-packed plant foods include soybeans (36g per cup), lentils (18g per cup), tempeh (31g per cup), edamame (17g per cup), quinoa (8g per cup), oats (6g per cup), peanut butter (16g per 2 Tbsp), pistachios (6g per oz), and spinach (5g per cup cooked). Leafy greens, broccoli, asparagus, artichokes, potatoes, whole grains and pseudograins are sources you might not expect. Variety ensures adequate protein.

In addition to choosing protein-rich plant staples, another helpful guideline is to include a source of protein in each meal and snack. Beans, tofu, tempeh, edamame, nuts, seeds, nut butters, and plant-based meats like seitan and veggie burgers can all make regular appearances. Starting your day with a tofu scramble, nut milk yogurt bowl, or protein-packed smoothie ensures you meet needs right from the start.

While protein needs can easily be met on plant-based diets through whole foods like beans, lentils, grains, nuts and seeds, you can also incorporate plant-based protein powders if desired for extra insurance. Pea protein, soy protein, hemp protein, and blends provide an additional 20-30 grams of protein per serving. Choose unflavored varieties without added sugars.

Contrary to popular belief, plant proteins are not inferior to animal proteins. All proteins are composed of the same twenty amino acids. Essential amino acids can only come from the diet, while non-essential ones can be made by the body. As long as you eat a sufficient calorie intake from varied plant sources, combining proteins in the same meal is unnecessary.

The Recommended Daily Allowance for protein is 0.8 grams per kilogram of body weight or about 10-15% of total daily calories. Active individuals may require more protein for muscle repair and growth. Plant-based diets can easily provide higher amounts for increased needs. With a balanced plant-based diet, protein should take care of itself.

In summary, whole food plant-based sources provide plentiful protein without the health risks linked to excess meat consumption. Dietary protein is readily available from beans, lentils, soy foods, nuts, seeds, whole grains, veggies, and plant-based meat alternatives. There is no need to micromanage protein intake or combine proteins in the same meal. Simply eating ample calories from diverse plants will effortlessly meet requirements. Banana

Calcium

Among the nutrients of concern for those adopting a plant-based diet, calcium often tops the list. Calcium plays vital roles including bone structure and strength, muscle and nerve function, and enzyme reactions. Low calcium intake over time can contribute to osteoporosis and fracture risk. However, it is a common myth that you need dairy products to get adequate calcium on a plant-based diet. In fact, calcium is abundant in a diverse array of plant foods, and vegans generally meet or exceed recommended intakes.

The RDA for calcium is 1000 mg per day for adults, increasing to 1200 mg per day for ages 50+. Optimal calcium intake supports bone mineral density, reducing the gradual bone loss associated with aging. Along with calcium, vitamin D and vitamin K2 also contribute to bone health and fracture prevention. Maintaining adequate calcium levels may also provide cognitive, cardiovascular and colon health benefits.

On a plant-based diet, leafy greens offer some of the best calcium sources. For instance, just one cup of cooked collard greens or kale provides over 250 mg calcium. Other top plant-based sources include calcium-set tofu, fortified plant milks and juices, beans, almonds, figs, tahini, tempeh, and broccoli. Seeds like chia, poppy, and sesame are also small but mighty calcium providers. Absorption is enhanced by pairing these foods with vitamin C-rich fruits or vegetables.

Studies consistently show vegans meet or exceed recommended calcium intakes. In the EPIC-Oxford study, vegans consumed the most calcium at an average of 1085 mg daily. This was higher than vegetarians or meat-eaters. Results from the Adventist Health Study-2 found the same trend, with vegans averaging 1142 mg daily. These observational findings illustrate that plant-based diets can sufficiently provide calcium through non-dairy sources.

Further research reveals vegans and vegetarians experience no greater risk of fractures compared to omnivores, despite low to nil milk intake. In a 2021 meta-analysis of 8 studies representing over 200,000 people, rates of hip, forearm and total fractures were similar regardless of diet pattern. A plant-based diet - when focused on calcium-rich foods - does not compromise bone health or increase fracture likelihood.

Tips for meeting calcium needs on a plant-based diet include:

- Enjoy greens like kale, broccoli, arugula, mustard and turnip greens daily. Beans and lentils are also great options.

- Consider a calcium-set tofu as a versatile non-dairy addition to meals.

- Choose fortified plant milks and juices as calcium-rich beverage options.

- Include chia seeds, tahini, almond butter, figs, and dried apricots for concentrated calcium.

- Consider a plant-based calcium supplement derived from algae if concerned about intakes.

With a balanced assortment of calcium-rich plant foods, those following vegan or vegetarian diets can meet their calcium needs for bone health. The notion that dairy is necessary for adequate calcium simply does not hold up to current evidence. A whole food plant-based diet offers plentiful bioavailable calcium sources to support your bone and body health.

Iron

Iron is an essential mineral that plays a vital role in many bodily functions. It is a key component of hemoglobin, enabling red blood cells to carry oxygen throughout the body. Iron is also necessary for energy metabolism, immune system function, brain development and more. Those switching to a plant-based diet sometimes worry about getting enough iron, but with the right foods and preparation tips, meeting needs on a vegan or vegetarian diet is totally achievable.

The recommended daily intake of iron is 8 mg for adult men and 18 mg for premenopausal women, to compensate for losses during menstruation. Iron deficiency is one of the most prevalent nutrient shortfalls, even among non-vegetarians. Symptoms include fatigue, weakness, pale skin and other indications of anemia. However getting sufficient iron on a plant-based eating plan is simple with a little nutrition know-how.

There are two forms of dietary iron - heme and non-heme. Heme iron, found only in meat and seafood, is absorbed at higher rates. Plant foods contain non-heme iron, which is more sensitive to inhibitors and enhancers of absorption. But there are many ways to optimize non-heme iron intake from vegetarian sources.

Eating foods high in vitamin C, like citrus fruits, peppers and broccoli, improves iron absorption substantially. Combining iron-rich foods with a vitamin C source in the same meal is an effective strategy. Foods high in beta-carotene such as carrots, sweet potatoes and spinach also boost iron absorption.

Meanwhile, compounds in coffee, tea, bran cereals, soybeans, and calcium supplements can hinder iron uptake when consumed in large amounts. Avoid drinking coffee or tea with meals if you are concerned about iron levels. However, moderate intake of these beverages is perfectly fine for most people.

Including plenty of iron-rich plant foods in your diet is key. Beans, lentils, tofu, nuts, seeds, oats, fortified cereals and dried fruit are all excellent choices. Leafy greens also supply some iron, as vitamin C aids absorption. Enriching meals with even small amounts of animal products like cheese can provide a heme iron boost.

Cooking with cast iron pots and pans adds trace iron to dishes. Opt for iron-fortified foods and beverages when possible - look for iron in the ingredients list. Sprouting and fermenting grains, beans and seeds increases their bioavailable iron content as well.

Those at risk for deficiency or concerned about levels can consider supplementing with a vegan iron product. Speak to your healthcare provider about whether this may be appropriate for you. Routinely having your blood work checked lets you monitor iron status.

Pairing plant-based iron sources thoughtfully in meals and snacks helps ensure optimal absorption. For breakfast, have oatmeal cooked in soy milk, topped with nuts and dried fruit, alongside citrus segments or juice. Or blenderize tofu, cocoa powder, berries and orange juice into a mineral-rich smoothie.

For lunch, whip up a hearty bean chili full of veggies, tomatoes and peppers. Or make a quinoa salad with edamame, nuts, dried cranberries and vinaigrette. Having hummus with carrot sticks and tomatoes also makes a good iron-boosting snack.

At dinner, stir-fry tofu and veggies in a cast iron wok and serve with a glass of enriched non-dairy milk. Or put together a hearty burrito bowl with beans, greens, rice, salsa and guacamole. Having berries with non-dairy yogurt for dessert provides vitamin C to enhance absorption.

As long as you eat a balanced, varied diet with sufficient calories and good sources of vitamin C, iron should naturally fall into place. Focus on getting your iron mainly from whole foods rather than supplements if possible. Aim to consume iron-rich choices multiple times throughout the day for steadier supply.

With a little knowledge and planning, plant-based eating can easily meet iron needs and prevent deficiency. The tips here will help you maximize this important mineral. Pairing plant foods strategically and cooking in iron-rich pots allows you to take advantage of the iron readily available in plant-based meal options.

Omega-3s

Omega-3 fatty acids provide vital benefits ranging from heart health to brain function. The most biologically active forms are EPA and DHA. With fish being a primary source of these omega-3s, it's common to wonder how plant-based eaters can obtain adequate amounts. Rest assured, there are effective ways to get anti-inflammatory omega-3 fats on a vegan or vegetarian diet.

Alpha-linolenic acid (ALA) is the plant-based form of omega-3. It's found abundantly in flaxseeds, chia seeds, hemp seeds, walnuts, and Brussels sprouts. Though less potent, ALA still offers protective effects for the cardiovascular system and brain health. The body can convert ALA into EPA and then DHA, but at fairly low rates. Between 5-10% of ALA converts to EPA, while only 1-5% becomes DHA.

Therefore, relying solely on ALA sources means you may fall short of ideal intakes for EPA and DHA. The adequate intake for ALA is 1.1 grams daily for women and 1.6 grams for men. For EPA/DHA, at least 250 milligrams per day is recommended. Vegans typically meet or exceed ALA needs simply by including flax, chia, walnuts and leafy greens regularly. But they average 62-184 mg of DHA daily - below suggested targets.

The good news is that practical solutions exist to close this gap:

- Increasing ALA intake from varied plant sources can help maximize EPA/DHA conversion rates. Enjoy omega-3 rich seeds daily, and add Brussels sprouts, avocado and leafy greens often.

- Pair ALA foods with vitamin C for greater conversion efficiency. Some options are citrus fruits, bell peppers, broccoli, strawberries and tomatoes.

- Reduce intake of omega-6s, as they compete metabolically with omega-3s. Limit oils high in omega-6 like corn, sunflower, cottonseed and safflower.

- If concerned about status, directly supplement with an algae-derived DHA/EPA supplement. Algae is the original source where fish obtain omega-3s.

- Consider eating DHA-rich sea vegetables like nori, dulse and kelp a few times a week.

- Choose fortified foods like plant milks, breakfast cereals, eggs and yogurt with added DHA.

- Eat more EPA/DHA-rich plant foods like sea buckthorn berries, edamame, kidney beans and mungo beans.

With a combination of these tips, plant-based eaters can meet their omega-3 fatty acid needs for supporting overall wellness. Aim for at least 2-3 grams of ALA per day, then supplement or boost DHA-rich foods to reach 250 milligrams of DHA. Those with heart disease risk factors, depression or pregnancy have greater DHA needs of at least 200-300 milligrams per day.

Ensuring adequate omega-3 intake does require more intention on a vegan diet compared to fish-inclusive diets. However, the plant kingdom offers diverse options, from ALA-rich seeds and nuts to sea vegetables and microalgae. With a little extra care selecting omega-3 foods or supplements, a plant-based lifestyle can absolutely meet EPA and DHA needs for optimal health.

Vitamin B12

Vitamin B12 is an essential nutrient that plays a crucial role in many body functions. It is necessary for healthy blood cells, DNA synthesis, energy production, and more. Since vitamin B12 is only found naturally in animal foods, vegans must supplement it or eat fortified foods. Getting enough vitamin B12 is critical on a plant-based diet, so this chapter covers how to obtain it from reliable plant sources.

Vitamin B12 keeps the nervous system functioning properly and helps form red blood cells. It is also needed to synthesize DNA and various neurochemicals. A long-term deficiency can lead to anemia, fatigue, neurological issues and mood changes. B12 is especially important for pregnant women, infants and the elderly.

On a standard Western diet including meat, dairy and eggs, vitamin B12 intake is typically adequate. But since it is only produced by microorganisms, plant foods do not provide an active form unless fortified. Strict vegans and vegetarians who avoid dairy and eggs must seek alternative B12 sources.

Fortunately, it is easy to get all the vitamin B12 you need from fortified foods and supplements formulated for vegans. Certain plant-based milks, breakfast cereals, nutritional yeast and meat analogs are enriched with vitamin B12. Reading labels helps identify products with added B12.

Taking a daily B12 supplement provides a consistent, reliable source. Supplements derived from bacteria, such as cyanocobalamin, are vegan-friendly. A typical dosage is around 25 mcg per day, or weekly doses of 2,000 mcg. Speak to a healthcare provider about your individual needs.

Since vitamin B12 is stored in the body, it can take years for deficiency to develop. But without adequate intake, levels will eventually drop, making routine supplementation important, especially for those who have been vegan long-term. Getting bloodwork done can help monitor your B12 status.

Here are some easy ways to get vitamin B12 from fortified plant foods or supplements:

- Take a B12 supplement with breakfast or drink fortified non-dairy milk.

- Use nutritional yeast, a deactivated yeast with a cheesy, nutty flavor, when cooking or on popped popcorn. Two tablespoons provides about 4 mcg B12.

- Choose a cereal enriched with B12 and vitamin D, topping it with B12-fortified plant milk.

- Check for added B12 in plant-based protein bars, burgers, meat alternatives like seitan or tempeh, and condiments like nutritional yeast sauce.

- For kids, provide fortified milk alternatives, nutritional yeast added to meals, and a chewable B12 supplement.

- Use a plant-based protein powder enriched with B12 in smoothies or shakes.

- Add a serving of fortified yogurt or plant milk to your daily diet, enjoying it with breakfast, snacks or dessert.

Getting a regular, adequate B12 supply is absolutely essential on a vegan diet, so be diligent about including fortified foods or taking supplements. Pairing foods can maximize absorption - having fortified nut milk in cereal, for example. Time supplements carefully with meals.

If opting for daily pills, combine with breakfast. For weekly large dose supplements, take after breakfast for optimal absorption. Speak to your doctor about your individual B12 needs and if bloodwork to assess levels may be wise.

Ensuring you get vitamin B12 from fortified plant sources or supplements is easy with a little planning. Don't rely solely on fermented foods like tempeh or seaweed for B12, as they are unreliable sources. Read labels diligently and consult your healthcare provider if have any concerns about deficiency.

With adequate, regular supplementation and consumption of fortified foods, plant eaters can easily satisfy their vitamin B12 requirements. Do your research and speak with experts to determine the right dosage and schedule for your needs. Meeting this essential nutrient need is simple with all the vegan-friendly options now available.

CHAPTER 3

STOCKING A PLANT-BASED PANTRY

Whole grains

Whole grains deliver an abundance of nutrition and health benefits that makes them a cornerstone of healthy plant-based eating. Refined grains like white rice, bread and pasta have the bran and germ removed, stripping away fiber, protein, and vitamins. Whole grains retain these essential nutrients, lending superior nutritional value.

Incorporating minimally processed whole grains ensures intake of all parts of the grain seed - the fiber-rich bran, energizing germ, and starchy endosperm. This provides antioxidants, B vitamins, minerals, phytochemicals, fiber, protein, and complex carbohydrates that refined grains lack.

Fiber is especially important, keeping digestion regular, controlling blood sugar, lowering cholesterol, maintaining satiety and healthy weight, and feeding beneficial gut bacteria. Whole grains are far more nutritionally complete and offer protection against chronic disease.

Delicious whole grain options abound. Hearty whole wheat and grains like rye, spelt, farro, bulgur, buckwheat, barley, oats, brown rice, quinoa, amaranth, corn, and millet can all be readily enjoyed on a plant-based diet. From breads and muffins to pilafs, risottos, porridges, and salads, the possibilities are endless.

Intact whole grains have a far lower glycemic index than refined carbs, keeping blood sugar stable rather than spiking and crashing levels. They provide lasting energy. As an added benefit, chewing whole grains thoroughly aids in dental health.

In terms of specific health protective effects, whole grains have proven benefits for heart health. The fiber binds cholesterol and eliminates it from the body, while also improving lipid profiles and blood pressure. Whole grains guard against metabolic syndrome and type 2 diabetes by improving insulin sensitivity and blood sugar control.

Their anti-inflammatory and antioxidant compounds help protect against cancer development, particularly colorectal cancers. The fiber keeps waste moving quickly through the digestive tract, limiting potential carcinogen contact. Whole grains also support neurological function and may help stave off dementia.

The bran in whole grains houses a compound called lignan that has phytoestrogen properties to potentially reduce risk of hormone-related cancers and osteoporosis. Whole grains also contain unique antioxidants like selenium and vitamin E.

Overall, diets rich in whole plant foods like whole grains, fruits, vegetables, nuts, seeds, and beans have tremendous synergistic health benefits. Whole grains paired with produce provides antioxidants and phytochemicals that are especially potent together.

The Recommended Daily Allowance of whole grains is 3-5 servings per day (minimum 48 grams). One serving equals 1 slice whole grain bread, 1/2 cup cooked grains or pasta, 1 ounce dry cereal, or 1/2 cup cooked cereal. Most people fall far short of this, with refined grains crowding out whole grains.

Making just a few simple substitutions helps increase whole grain intake. Choose 100% whole wheat bread and pasta, brown rice over white, rolled or steel-cut oats instead of processed sweetened cereals. Explore less common ancient grains like amaranth, millet, sorghum and teff for texture and nutrient diversity.

Read labels carefully, as many products misleadingly claim "made with whole grains" while containing mostly refined flour with small whole grain amounts. Look for "100% whole grain" as the first ingredient. Avoid added sugars or oils.

Baking with 100% whole wheat flour gives control over ingredients. Soaking, sprouting or fermenting grains prior to cooking enhances digestibility and nutrient absorption. Give homemade granola, granola bars, crackers or bread a try.

Don't be intimidated by the thought of cooking whole grains like farro, barley and quinoa. They're simple to prepare by boiling like rice or oatmeal. Add savory herbs and spices, nuts or seeds for extra flavor and protein.

Grate raw grains in a food processor to make couscous for salads and bowls or as a breakfast porridge cooked in milk. Toss cooked grains with roasted veggies and beans or stuff into avocados or peppers.

With a little creativity, you will come to love nourishing whole grains and the variety and nutrition they offer. They provide the base for countless plant-based breakfasts, lunches, dinners and snacks. Your health will reap the benefits.

Legumes

Beans, lentils, peas and peanuts - collectively known as legumes - are nutritional powerhouses with an array of health benefits. Abundant in protein, fiber, vitamins and minerals, legumes offer key nourishment for those following plant-based eating patterns. Incorporating a variety of legumes regularly is recommended to meet nutritional needs while promoting optimal wellbeing.

With approximately 15g protein per cooked cup, beans and lentils are a superior plant-based protein source. This makes them ideal for vegans, vegetarians, and anyone seeking to reduce meat consumption. Bean proteins are high in lysine, complementing grains that are higher in methionine. Consuming beans with grains, nuts or corn provides complete protein with all essential amino acids.

Legumes are also exceptionally high in soluble and insoluble fiber. A single cup of cooked beans provides up to 75% of the recommended daily fiber intake. Soluble fibers help regulate cholesterol and blood sugar, while insoluble fibers promote healthy digestion and feed beneficial gut bacteria. Increased fiber intake reduces heart disease risk and assists with healthy weight maintenance.

In addition to protein and fiber, legumes supply key vitamins and minerals like iron, zinc, potassium, magnesium and folate. They are a concentrated source of polyphenols and other antioxidant phytochemicals that fight inflammation and oxidative stress. Red, orange, black and speckled beans are particularly rich in these protective plant compounds.

Incorporating more legumes offers additional benefits including:

- Lower LDL cholesterol and blood pressure
- Regulation of blood glucose levels
- Reduced colorectal cancer risk
- Increased satiety between meals
- Prevention of anemia due to high iron content
- Feeding of healthy gut microbiome

The dietary guidelines recommend 1.5 to 2 cups of legumes per week as part of a healthy diet. The optimal preparation methods are sprouting, soaking, fermenting and slow-cooking legumes to maximize nutrient absorption and digestion. Canned beans offer convenience, but may have higher sodium content. Rinsing and draining canned beans helps reduce excess sodium.

There are endless possibilities for enjoying beans, lentils, chickpeas and peas in plant-based cuisine. They pair well with grains like rice, quinoa, pasta and bread. Mash beans into dips, spreads or burger patties. Add lentils to soups, salads and casseroles. Blend white beans into creamy sauces. Roast chickpeas for a protein-rich snack. The flavors and textures of legumes serve as a versatile base for meals.

With their stellar nutritional profile, legumes belong in regular rotation for plant-based diets. Aim for 1-2 servings of beans, lentils or peas daily to benefit from their protein, fiber, vitamins, minerals and antioxidants. This legume-rich pattern supports cardiovascular and gastrointestinal health for optimal wellbeing.

Nuts and seeds

Nuts and seeds are nutritional powerhouses that offer immense health benefits. They provide ample protein, healthy fats, fiber, vitamins, minerals and antioxidants. That's why they are essential pantry staples on a well-rounded plant-based diet. This chapter will overview the nutritional perks of nuts and seeds, how to eat and prepare them, and the best choices to have on hand.

To start, nuts and seeds are a prime plant-based source of protein, making them a handy snack or meal addition. Almonds, pistachios, peanuts, cashews, pumpkin seeds, sunflower seeds and nut butters all contain substantial amounts of protein per serving. Hemp seeds are especially protein-packed, with a whopping 10g per ounce.

Plant foods often lack omega-3 fatty acids, but walnuts, chia seeds, hemp seeds and flaxseeds provide alpha-linolenic acid, or ALA, an anti-inflammatory omega-3. They also deliver heart-healthy monounsaturated fat. However, enjoy nuts and seeds in moderation since they are calorie-dense.

Fiber is another major benefit of these foods. One ounce of almonds has about 4g of belly-filling fiber, while a tablespoon of chia or flax seeds boasts 7-9g. This aids digestion, gut health and stable blood sugar. The crunchiness of nuts can also help satisfy when craving chips or crackers.

Further, nuts and seeds supply important vitamins and minerals like vitamin E, magnesium, calcium and iron. They also contain antioxidant compounds that fight free radical damage. Research links regular consumption to decreased inflammation and lower risks of chronic diseases.

When buying nuts and seeds, choose unsalted raw varieties without added oils or sweeteners. Read ingredients lists, as many roasted nuts are cooked in undesirable oils. Stick to plain, all-natural nuts in their whole form, not pieces, for maximum nutrition.

Refrigerating nuts and seeds keeps their healthy fats from oxidizing and prevents rancidity. But they should not be stored in the freezer. Transfer what you'll use within a week or two into an airtight container at room temperature.

To save money, buy in bulk from bins at health food stores, then divide into reasonable portions at home and freeze until needed. Toasting or roasting plain raw nuts intensifies their flavor.

There are countless easy ways to eat nuts and seeds or add them to recipes:

- Sprinkle onto oatmeal, cereal, yogurt or salad
- Whir into smoothies, sauces and dressings
- Bake into granola bars, cookies and other treats
- Fold into pancake, waffle or muffin batters
- Coat fish or tofu with crushed nuts before baking
- Add textural crunch to roasted veggies or rice dishes
- Enjoy nut butters on toast, with apples or on pancakes

Chia seeds are unique in that they create a gel when soaked in liquid. Use them to make puddings, breakfast bowls, vegan jams, and even egg replacements by soaking 1 tablespoon seeds in 3 tablespoons water. Ground flax seeds mixed with water work similarly.

However you enjoy them, having nuts and seeds regularly can do wonders for overall nutrition. They satisfy cravings for crunch and rich flavor in a plant-powered way. Just watch portions, as they are easy to overeat. Focus on raw, unsalted varieties over heavily processed and flavored options when possible.

Nuts and seeds are highly versatile nutritional assets. With a little creativity, they can be incorporated into sweet and savory recipes alike or simply snacks on as-is. Keeping a variety on hand makes whipping up balanced plant-based meals easier. Your health will reap the benefits of these mighty "little" superfoods.

Spices and seasonings

Spices and herbs are the unsung heroes in any vegan kitchen. They add vibrant flavor to dishes without fat, sugar or salt. Maximizing use of aromatic spices and herbs is key to creating delicious plant-based meals.

Common spices like cumin, turmeric, cinnamon, coriander, curry powder, paprika, saffron, ginger and chili pepper can transform a basic vegetable dish into something irresistible. Herbs like basil, cilantro, parsley, rosemary, oregano, dill, thyme and mint brighten up grains, beans, soups and salads.

Spices come from the root, bark, fruit, seeds or flowers of plants grown around the world. Each has its own flavor profile, aromatic compounds and health enhancing effects. Many provide antioxidants, anti-inflammatories and antimicrobial properties.

Learning how to pair spices and foods is essential for satisfying plant-based cooking. Warm spices like cinnamon, nutmeg, cumin, turmeric, coriander, curry and chili pepper enhance starchy vegetables like sweet potatoes, squash, carrots and beets. Cooler herbs like mint, cilantro and parsley nicely complement beans, greens and summertime produce.

Don't be afraid to experiment with new spice combinations. Curries using turmeric, coriander, cumin and ginger are versatile. Italian herbs like basil, oregano and parsley liven up marinara sauce. Smoked paprika adds richness to stews and tacos. Saffron threads make aromatic rice. Always adjust amounts to taste and find your perfect balance.

In addition to flavor, many spices confer health benefits. Turmeric contains the anti-inflammatory compound curcumin. Garlic and onions contain immunity-boosting allicin. Ginger is a soothing nausea reliever. Cinnamon helps regulate blood sugar. Black pepper's piperine boosts absorption of nutrients.

Going beyond the spice rack, chilies and hot sauces bring heat and endorphins. Jalapenos, habaneros, cayenne, chipotle and ancho peppers add zest. Vinegars, mustards, horseradish, wasabi and ginger also provide a kick. Use spicy seasonings to taste. They boost metabolism and have antibiotic potential.

When possible, purchase high-quality spices in smaller quantities and replace them regularly for the best flavor. Store spices in airtight containers away from heat and light to preserve volatile oils. Buy whole seeds like cumin and coriander and grind them just before using.

Double-down on flavor with these tips: Bloom spices in oil to intensify aroma before adding other ingredients. Roast whole spices briefly before grinding. Add spices to dishes at different stages. Finish with fresh herbs. Play sweet and spicy contrasts off each other.

Composing a global spice collection is one of the joys of plant-based cooking. Start with familiar spices and pick one or two new ones to try each time you shop. Soon you'll have an arsenal to whip up Indian curries, Moroccan tagines, Cajun jambalaya, jerk Caribbean beans, zesty Mexican quinoa and more.

Homemade spice blends save money and let you control ingredients. Whip up hearty blends like garam masala, ras el hanout, or Italian seasoning to have on hand. Make chili powder by mixing ground spices like cumin, oregano, paprika, garlic and cayenne.

Spice pastes open up more possibilities. Blend ginger, garlic, chilies and herbs with oil for stir fry sauces. Massage spice pastes onto proteins before cooking. Whip up flavored oils and vinegars to drizzle. Mix tahini, spices and citrus for dressing. The options are endless.

The beauty of spices is their versatility. A base stew can become completely different meals with creative blends: Indian with cumin, coriander and garam masala or Ethiopian with berbere powder and paprika. Spices satisfy cravings for rich flavors without adding significant calories.

Make the flavors in plant-based dishes explode by fully utilizing the potential of aromatic spices and herbs. Curate your own collection to suit your palate. With an arsenal of spices, you can create round-the-world plant-based cuisine full of depth, complexity and health benefits. The result will be mouthwatering meals that even spice-loving carnivores will drool over.

Oils

While whole food sources of fats should take center stage in plant-based eating, oils can have an appropriate supporting role for flavor and texture. Oils are 100% fat, extracted from various plant foods like seeds, nuts, and fruits. Choosing the right oils and using restraint helps tap their culinary utility without excess.

Oils offer monounsaturated and polyunsaturated fats that provide health benefits in moderation. High quality oils also contribute antioxidant compounds like vitamin E. However, all oils are extremely calorie-dense, providing 120 calories per tablespoon. For optimal health, it's best to rely on whole food sources of fats like avocados, nuts, seeds and olives whenever possible. Minimize extracted oils for flavoring or occasional cooking.

The most suitable oils for a plant-based diet include:

- Extra Virgin Olive Oil: High in monounsaturated fat and phenolic antioxidants. Ideal for dressings, marinades and light sautéing.

- Avocado Oil: Rich source of monounsaturated fats with a mild flavor. Good for baking or medium-heat cooking.

- Walnut Oil: Delivers a dose of anti-inflammatory omega-3 ALA. Best used unheated in dressings or sauces.

- Sesame Oil: Strongly flavored oil providing vitamin E. Use sparingly to add nutty essence to dishes.

- Coconut Oil: With a high smoke point, coconut oil withstands higher heat. Provides lauric acid and MCTs. Use minimally.

Oils to use very sparingly or avoid include corn, cottonseed, soybean, grapeseed, sunflower and safflower oils. Though high in polyunsaturates, they are often highly processed and pro-inflammatory.

When cooking with oil, use just enough to lightly coat the pan or food. Limit deep frying. Measure salad dressings and sauces carefully; a little oil goes a long way for flavor. Consider diluting dressings with equal parts water or vinegar to reduce oil quantity.

For homemade baked goods, limit added fats to no more than 2-3 tablespoons per recipe. Applesauce, mashed banana, avocado, nut butters or soaked nuts can replace some or all oil in many recipes. Boost flavor with spices, extracts and zest instead of extra oil.

Overall, emphasize whole food sources of healthy fats like nuts, seeds, avocados, olives and their butters. Think of oils as optional flavor enhancers, not dietary necessities. Prioritize antioxidant-rich extra virgin olive and avocado oil. With mindful use of plant-based oils, you can meet your daily fat intake from predominantly whole food nutrition.

Sweeteners

When transitioning to a plant-based diet, you may need to find alternatives for conventional refined sugars. Luckily, nature provides many healthier sweetener options perfect for vegan baking and reducing reliance on processed sugars. This chapter explores natural plant-based sweeteners, how to use them, and their nutritional pros and cons.

First, let's examine why overusing typical white and brown sugars is problematic. Table sugar has no nutrients and overconsumption can lead to weight gain, blood sugar spikes, inflammation, and fatty liver disease. Refined sugars also feed harmful gut bacteria. But small amounts of natural sweeteners can satisfy cravings when used thoughtfully.

Plant-derived sweeteners provide more nutrients and health benefits versus conventional options. Most have a lower glycemic index, meaning they do not spike blood sugar as dramatically. However, they are still considered added sugars and should be used in moderation. Here are some top choices:

Maple Syrup – Made from boiled sap of maple trees, maple syrup contains antioxidants and minerals like zinc and potassium. It has high levels of iron compared to other sweeteners, at 5%

DV per tablespoon. Look for 100% pure grades. Use it on pancakes, oatmeal, or to sweeten sauces.

Molasses – A byproduct of refining sugarcane into table sugar, molasses is thick and syrupy with bold flavor. It supplies iron, calcium, magnesium, and potassium. Use blackstrap molasses for maximum nutrition. Add to baked goods, barbecue sauces, stews, or even smoothies.

Dates – Dried, pitted dates can be substituted for refined sugar in recipes. They are high in fiber, potassium, magnesium and antioxidants. Soak dates to blend into smoothies or puree into sweet sauces, energy bites or baked goods. Replace 1 cup sugar with 1 cup chopped dates.

Raw Local Honey – Unpasteurized honey contains enzymes, antioxidants, minerals, and antibacterial properties. Use in moderation, as it still has a high sugar content. Honey is not vegan but can be part of a plant-based diet. Add to tea, yogurt, oatmeal, or bake into desserts.

Stevia – Stevia comes from a South American plant. The extracted sweet compounds like Stevioside and Rebaudioside A are zero-calorie and 200-400x sweeter than sugar. Note some commercial products combine stevia with artificial sweeteners. Use drops of the liquid extract or powder to lightly sweeten drinks, yogurt, cereal and baked goods.

Monk Fruit – Also called Luo Han Guo, monk fruit is native to China. It contains zero calories and is 150-200 times sweeter than sugar. The sweetness comes from antioxidants called mogrosides. Use monk fruit extract powder or liquid to lightly sweeten beverages, yogurt, cereals, smoothies and desserts.

Coconut Sugar – Made from dehydrated coconut palm sap, coconut sugar has a slight caramel flavor. It contains fiber, protein, potassium, iron, zinc, and antioxidants. Use in place of brown sugar in recipes due to its brown hue and nutrients. Sugars are still sugars, so use all sweeteners, even "natural" ones, in moderation. But plant-based options are generally less processed and provide more health benefits.

When baking, you can often reduce added sweeteners by 25% from what a recipe calls for, since whole foods like fruit or chocolate provide sweetness too. Some plant-based milk and yogurt brands have added sugar, so compare nutrition labels to choose unsweetened varieties whenever possible.

Enjoying the natural flavors fruits - from bananas, berries, apples, pineapple, and more - is an easy way to satisfy a sweet tooth with less added sugars. Dried fruits especially pack concentrated sweetness. Overall, sticking to mainly whole foods and water or unsweetened tea and coffee as your drinks limits sugar intake substantially.

With a toolkit of plant-based sweeteners, you can continue to enjoy sweet flavors on a vegan diet without relying on refined table sugar. Use alternatives like maple syrup and dates in moderation, focusing on getting nutrients from wholesome, minimally processed foods. Your taste buds and health will thank you.

CHAPTER 4
ENERGIZING BREAKFASTS

Smoothies

Smoothies make for quick, nutritious breakfasts and snacks that are endlessly customizable. Blending together fruits, veggies, nuts, seeds and liquid creates a portable meal or beverage loaded with vitamins, minerals and antioxidants. Smoothies are an ideal way to pack more produce into your diet.

The base of a balanced smoothie is fruit, which provides sweetness and nutrients. Berries, bananas, mangos, pineapple, apples, pears, peaches, cherries and citrus fruits all make tasty bases. Fruit balances out stronger flavored ingredients.

Leafy greens build nutritional value, as do nutrient-dense vegetables like carrots, sweet potatoes and beets. Spinach, kale, swiss chard, romaine and arugula add vitamins without overpowering fruit flavor.

Non-dairy milks create creaminess and are more nutritious than juice or water alone. Almond, coconut, soy, oat and hemp milks provide protein. Avoid sugary fruit juices, which spike blood sugar without fiber's benefits.

Healthy fats make smoothies rich, satisfying and heart healthy. Options like avocado, nut or seed butters, flaxseed, chia seeds and coconut provide essential fatty acids and creaminess. Protein powders boost nutrition further.

Herbs, spices and natural sweeteners customize smoothie flavors. Vanilla, cinnamon, cocoa powder, fresh ginger and mint perk up tastes. Dates, raw honey or maple syrup lend sweetness if desired. Ice cubes chill while bananas or avocado freeze nicely too.

Smoothie ratios depend on your goals. Fruit-based versions are tasty treats. Equal fruit and greens makes a balanced meal. More veggies and protein turn it into a muscle-building drink. Cater recipes to your needs.

Some toothsome flavor combos include:

- Berry - strawberries, blueberries, raspberries, cherries with banana, Greek yogurt, milk, cinnamon
- Green machine - kale, spinach, mango, pineapple, coconut water, lime
- Carrot cake - carrots, pineapple, banana, walnuts, cinnamon, nutmeg, vanilla
- Chocolate peanut butter - banana, cacao powder, peanut butter, milk, dates
- Nuts and seeds - strawberries, almond butter, ground flax, chia seeds, almond milk
- Tropical - pineapple, mango, coconut milk, lime, ginger, vanilla

Smoothies make ideal breakfasts to power your day. Blend portable batches you can grab on the go. They also satisfy sweet cravings in a healthy way. Use after workouts to refuel and build muscle with added protein.

Get creative with combinations that pack in anti-inflammatory, antioxidant-rich fruits and veggies. Change up flavors based on seasonal produce and what you have on hand.

Making smoothies is fast, easy clean up and allows for endless variations. Use high-speed blenders like Vitamix to pulverize ingredients, especially leafy greens. Start with wet ingredients, then add fruits, greens and powders. Blend until smooth.

Smoothies keep in the refrigerator 2-3 days, though some separation occurs. You can blend again before drinking. Freeze batch leftovers in popsicle molds for healthy fudgesicles.

Drink smoothies immediately for best texture and flavor. If too thick, thin with water or milk to desired consistency. Top with fresh fruit, dried coconut, cacao nibs, chia seeds or nut butter for garnish.

Overflowing with fruits, vegetables, nuts and seeds, smoothies provide the perfect opportunity to pack extra nutrition into your plant-based diet. Their versatility makes them ideal go-to breakfasts, snacks, desserts or workout fuels. Power up your blends with superfood additions like maca, hemp seeds, cacao and more. Indulge your creativity to whip up the perfect smoothie for health in a glass! Banana

Overnight oats

Overnight oats have become a staple easy plant-based breakfast. By soaking oats and mix-ins in liquid overnight, the oats soften into a creamy, pudding-like texture while still retaining their chew. The possibilities for customizing overnight oats are endless, making them a perfect weekday breakfast.

Overnight oats provide sustained energy with complex carbohydrates, fiber, protein, and healthy fats to power you through the morning. Steel cut or old fashioned oats work best, as they hold their shape and texture better than quick oats. Feel free to use gluten-free oats if avoiding gluten.

The basic formula is 1/2 cup uncooked oats to 1 cup liquid. Water, plant-based milk, juice and yogurt all work. Use a container with a lid to mix and refrigerate overnight, at least 5-6 hours. The oats will absorb the liquid as they soak. Add extras like fruits, nuts, seeds, nut butter, spices, etc. to customize the flavors.

Here are some tasty overnight oats combinations to try:

Apple Pie – Dice apples and add cinnamon, maple syrup or dates, raisins, chopped walnuts. Use almond milk and top with nut butter.

Chocolate Peanut Butter – Add cocoa powder and peanut butter or powder. Banana slices or berries pair nicely.

Carrot Cake – Grate carrots into the oats. Add cinnamon, nutmeg, raisins and walnuts with almond milk.

Piña Colada – Use coconut milk and diced pineapple. Sprinkle shredded coconut on top.

Pumpkin Spice – Mix in canned pumpkin puree, pumpkin pie spice, vanilla and maple syrup.

Mocha – Brew coffee or espresso to use instead of water. Add cocoa powder, chocolate chips, a splash of coffee liqueur.

Blueberry Muffin – Fold in fresh or frozen blueberries. Add vanilla and lemon zest, using almond milk.

Strawberries & Cream – Mash fresh strawberries into the oats. Top with coconut cream yogurt.

Tropical Fruit – Use pineapple, mango and banana. Sprinkle with shredded coconut.

PB & J – Swirl in peanut butter and your favorite jam, adding milk and a pinch of salt.

Chia seeds, ground flax, hemp seeds, nuts and nut butters increase protein and healthy fats. Mix in nutritious boosters like cocoa powder, chia seeds, bee pollen or collagen peptides.

For added texture, fold in granola or muesli. Cooked quinoa or brown rice bring even more whole grains. Shredded vegetables like zucchini or carrots also work nicely.

Dress up your oats with toppings like sliced fruit, toasted nuts or seeds, plant-based yogurt, nut butter, jam, maple syrup or agave. Ground cinnamon, cardamom, pumpkin pie spice and vanilla extract lend warmth.

Make a batch on Sunday to have easy, grab-and-go breakfasts for the week. Overnight oats keep 3-5 days refrigerated. Mason jars or compartments make transport easy.

The basic method scales up or down easily. Use 1/4 cup oats per serving. Overnight oats are highly versatile, so get creative with mix-ins. Savory versions with spices, greens and sautéed veggies are also delicious.

No need to heat overnight oats, but you can reheat briefly or enjoy chilled. Kids love being able to customize their own flavors. Boost nutrition with superfood powders, wheat germ or ground flax.

Some other quick tips for overnight oats success:

- Use thicker, non-dairy yogurts for more creaminess.
- Try different milks like soy, oat, coconut or almond.
- Make a batch then divide into individual portions to flavor later.
- Avoid mushiness by not oversoaking; 6-8 hours max.
- Rinse oats to prevent sliminess if not using dairy milk.
- Refrigerate in warm months or if your kitchen is warm.

Overnight oats offer endless possibilities for plant-based breakfast. They're budget-friendly, satisfying and full of whole food nutrition. Meal prep overnight oats on the weekend for easy mornings. Keep your grains interesting by trying new flavors!

Pancakes and waffles

Pancakes and waffles are beloved breakfast treats that can certainly be enjoyed on a plant-based diet. With the right substitutions and techniques, you can create fluffy, flavorful versions made from nourishing whole grain flours, plant-based milks and natural sweeteners. Satisfy your weekend breakfast cravings without sacrificing nutrition.

When adapting traditional recipes, replace the eggs with "flax eggs" - a mixture of ground flaxseed and water that mimics the binding action of eggs. Use 1 tablespoon ground flax + 3 tablespoons water per egg called for. Let the mixture rest briefly to thicken. Applesauce, mashed banana or aquafaba can also substitute for eggs in pancake and waffle batters.

For the dairy milk, opt for unsweetened almond, soy, oat or coconut milk beverages. When choosing plant-based milk, avoid sweetened vanilla flavors and seek out higher protein options.

The milk helps add moisture as well as flavor. Non-dairy yogurt also works well in place of regular dairy yogurt or buttermilk.

In terms of flour, try combinations of whole wheat or white whole wheat flour with gluten-free flours. Good choices are oat flour, almond flour, coconut flour, or chickpea flour. These provide binding power and texture. A small amount of all-purpose flour can be used too. Baking powder and salt help the batters rise and brown.

Natural sweeteners like maple syrup, coconut sugar, fruit juice or mashed ripe banana lend sweetness with added nutrition. Reduce any added sugars to keep the glycemic impact in check. Vanilla and citrus zest also help enhance flavor.

Nuts, seeds, nut butters or chopped fruit make tasty mix-in options. Try walnuts, pecans, almonds, sunflower seeds, flaxseeds, peanut butter, almond butter, berries, bananas, apples or plant-based chocolate chips.

Oil is necessary for moisture and texture, but use sparingly. Canola, grapeseed, sunflower or melted coconut oil are good choices. If you have a high-powered blender, you can try blending soaked nuts like cashews, macadamia nuts or almonds into a cream to replace the oil.

Key tips for plant-based pancakes and waffles:

- Allow flax egg mixtures to thicken for at least 5 minutes
- Avoid overmixing the batter
- Use coconut oil spray on the griddle or waffle iron
- Flip pancakes after bubbles appear on surface
- Adjust batter consistency as needed with more milk or flour
- Add mix-ins just before cooking for evenly dispersed goodness

With a few simple ingredient swaps, you can certainly enjoy fluffy vegan pancakes and waffles without compromising your healthy plant-based diet. Turn your Sunday mornings into a delightful, comforting ritual.

Tofu scrambles

Tofu scrambles are a vegetarian staple that mimic the fluffy, protein-packed texture of egg scrambles. Using crumbled tofu and flavorful spices and vegetables, it's easy to whip up a plant-based scramble bursting with nutrition.

Tofu provides a neutral base with a similar egg-like texture once crumbled. Firm or extra firm tofu works best to provide structure that won't get mushy during cooking. Drain and press tofu to remove excess water before using.

To crumble, simply squeeze the block of tofu between your hands over a bowl, breaking it into small, bite-sized pieces. You can also pulse chunks briefly in a food processor. The crumbles should resemble scrambled egg texture.

Cooking the tofu scramble is done just like eggs. Heat a skillet over medium with a bit of oil or broth. Add the crumbled tofu and sauté until starting to turn golden brown around the edges.

Stirring frequently prevents sticking and allows moisture to evaporate for a fluffier texture. Cook 5-10 minutes until heated through. You can make this step ahead and reheat later.

Once the crumbled tofu base is cooked, add in diced vegetables and spices. Onion, bell pepper, mushrooms, tomatoes, spinach, kale and zucchini all make excellent mix-ins.

Chopped veggies add color, texture, nutrients and flavor. Cook until softened but still bright in color.

Spices and seasoning transform the scramble. Turmeric provides the iconic egg shade. Nutritional yeast lends a savory, cheesy umami taste. Salt, pepper, garlic and onion powder or fresh herbs season to taste.

Sauté everything together for a few minutes to let flavors mingle. Taste and adjust salt, pepper or other spices as needed.

Finally, a splash of non-dairy milk or creamer right at the end gives a lovely creamy finish. Stir this in and heat just until warmed through.

Simple toast or cooked potatoes turn the scramble into a hearty breakfast. Plus, tofu scrambles make easy, protein and nutrient-packed dinners too.

Get creative with mix-in ingredients like sautéed peppers, spinach, mushrooms and tomatoes. Black salt adds extra egg flavor. Stir in pesto or salsa for a twist.

Here are some tasty flavor combos to try:

- Southwest - onion, bell pepper, salsa, cumin, cayenne, cilantro
- Greens and mushrooms - garlic, shallot, spinach, kale, mushrooms
- Mediterranean - artichokes, sun-dried tomatoes, basil, olives
- Tex Mex - onion, jalapeno, chili powder, garlic, cumin
- Indian curry - onion, carrot, curry powder, garlic, ginger
- Breakfast - onion, potato, pepper, nutritional yeast, turmeric

Don't limit yourself to breakfast. Turn scrambles into fabulous sandwiches and wraps. Stuff into pita or sandwich with hummus, lettuce, tomato and avocado.

Meal prep batches of scrambled tofu crumbles to reheat during your week. They keep well for 2-3 days refrigerated and are easy grab and go breakfasts or snacks.

Get the whole family loving healthy tofu scrambles. Make weekend brunch special with a build your own toppings bar. Set out diced veggies, sauces and seasonings for everyone to customize.

Bursting with nutrition from vegetables and spice, protein-packed tofu scrambles will satisfy comfort food cravings in a healthy plant-based way. Let creativity run wild with global spice blends and veggie mix-ins. Enjoy a new scramble every day of the week!

Breakfast burritos

Breakfast burritos are a deliciously convenient plant-based meal any time of day. Fluffy scrambled tofu or beans, veggies, savory sauces and spices are all wrapped in a warm tortilla for on-the-go enjoyment. Endlessly customizable, breakfast burritos are easy to make in batches and freeze too. This chapter will explore creative fillings, tortilla options and simple cook methods to start your day with these hearty handhelds.

At its simplest, a breakfast burrito contains eggs, cheese and meat wrapped in a flour tortilla. But using tofu, beans, or veggie crumbles instead creates a satisfying plant-based version. Large burritos make a complete meal, while smaller ones are nice for snacking.

With so many possible fillings, part of the fun is trying new combinations! Crumbled or scrambled tofu, mashed black beans, or soyrizo seasoned with taco spices are easy protein replacements for ground meat.

From there, add any sautéed or roasted veggies you enjoy - potatoes, bell peppers, mushrooms, kale, spinach, etc. Rice, beans, avocado, salsa, vegan cheese, caramelized onions and peppers all mix in wonderfully too.

Some tasty breakfast burrito fillings to inspire you:

- Tofu "egg" scramble with peppers, onions, spinach, salsa and avocado
- Roasted sweet potatoes, black beans, salsa, spinach and vegan sour cream
- Brown rice, refried beans, sautéed zucchini and corn, grated vegan cheese
- Crispy potatoes and onion, mushrooms, tofu scramble, guacamole
- Soyrizo, potato, bell pepper, onion, cilantro, pickled jalapenos

- Lentils, sautéed mushrooms and chard, sun-dried tomatoes, basil
- Chickpeas, roasted broccoli and cauliflower, vegan pesto, parsley

The tortilla is key for keeping these burritos together. Flour and corn tortillas are common. Warm them before filling to make them pliable and prevent cracking.

Corn tortillas have a lovely soft texture and sweet flavor. 100% sprouted grain or gluten-free tortillas are other options. Smaller tortillas make burritos easier to eat by hand.

Once you have your desired fillings, assemble the burritos using these steps:

- Warm the tortillas in the microwave or oven so they are flexible.
- Place fillings across the center of the tortilla, leaving room at the edges to fold. Don't overstuff.
- Fold the bottom edge of the tortilla over the filling, then tightly roll up the sides.
- Place the burrito seam side down on the plate to keep it together.

Add any sauces, salsa or guacamole you're using on top or with the fillings. Burritos hold together best when the tortilla is warm and pliable. Rice, beans or roasted veggies help bind the ingredients too.

Meal prepping breakfast burritos makes busy mornings so much easier. Make a big batch over the weekend and freeze them. To reheat from frozen, remove foil and place in a 300F oven for 20-25 minutes until hot and toasty. The tortilla will crisp slightly.

You can also refrigerate assembled burritos up to 5 days or keep the components separate and assemble as needed. Reheat refrigerated burritos in the microwave. Add all your favorite Tex-Mex flavors and make this plant-powered breakfast your own!

CHAPTER 5
SATISFYING LUNCHES

Salads

Salads make the perfect plant-based meal or side, offering a tasty way to pack in the veggies. With a bed of greens and rainbow of add-ins, salads provide color, crunch, and fresh flavor. Take your salads from bland to brilliant with creative combinations and smart techniques.

Start your salad with a base of mixed greens like spinach, kale, arugula, lettuce or cabbage. Branch out beyond lettuce to take advantage of unique textures and nutrients. Massaged kale, roasted broccoli and shredded Brussels sprouts also make excellent salad bases.

When choosing produce add-ins, include a variety of colors for a spectrum of vitamins and antioxidants. Red tomatoes, orange carrots, yellow peppers, purple cabbage, green cucumbers and more. Roast vegetables to bring out new depths of sweetness. Fresh herbs like basil, cilantro or parsley lend brightness.

For a protein boost, sprinkle on beans, lentils, tofu, tempeh, edamame or nuts/seeds. Chickpeas, kidney beans and cannellini beans pair well with green salads. Hearty lentils or baked tofu can transform a salad into an entrée. Nutritional yeast is a dairy-free substitute for cheese with B-vitamins.

Dress your salad with healthy fats for flavor and absorption of fat-soluble nutrients. Options like olive oil, hemp seeds, sunflower seeds, avocado and olives add richness. Nut-based oils offer creamy texture.

For the dressing, make your own using oil, vinegar/citrus juice, herbs and spices. Apple cider, balsamic, white wine or rice vinegar provide tang. Lemon, lime or orange juice also deliver bright notes. Whisk in dried oregano, basil, thyme or cumin.

Or use store-bought dressings sparingly, watch for added sugar. Seek out oil-free hummus, tahini or nut butter based dressings for creaminess without excess oil.

Eat salad dressings on the side or use just enough to lightly coat. Cut oil and calories by mixing dressing with equal parts water or broth.

For topping crunch, try nuts, crispy roasted chickpeas, sunflower seeds, roasted beet strips, croutons, tortilla strips, puffed quinoa or toasted nori. Sprinkle just before eating to stay crispy.

With the right base, mix-ins, dressing and toppings, you can create diverse flavor-packed salads as part of your healthy plant-based diet.

Soups and stews

Soups and stews are nourishing one-pot meals perfect for going plant-based. Simply chop vegetables, add beans or grain for protein, simmer until tender and season to taste - easy homemade comfort food!

The base begins with aromatics like onion, garlic, celery, carrots and peppers for depth of flavor. Sautéing them briefly before adding liquid intensifies the taste. Tomato product and potatoes lend thickness as well.

Sturdy veggies suitable for simmering work well: potatoes, carrots, parsnips, turnips, sweet potatoes, pumpkin, cauliflower, broccoli, mushrooms, squash, greens, etc. Chop any veggies into bite-sized pieces so they cook evenly.

Beans cooked from scratch or canned provide protein, fiber and texture. Try any variety - navy, kidney, great northern, lentils, chickpeas, black beans or edamame. If using canned, rinse before adding. Grains like barley, farro or quinoa make hearty additions too.

For liquid, vegetable broth or stock builds maximum flavor. If using water, add a splash of white wine or lemon juice to brighten. Tomato juice, puree or diced tomatoes add richness. Non-dairy milks work too, but avoid adding before simmering as they may curdle.

Herbs and spices bring layers of flavor. Basil, parsley, thyme, oregano, rosemary, cumin, paprika, chili powder and garlic are excellent seasoning options. Season modestly at first then adjust to taste after cooking.

Simmer soups and stews until vegetables are fork tender, 30-60 minutes usually. The longer the simmer, the more the flavors develop and meld. Stir occasionally and add a bit more broth as needed if reducing too much.

When veggies are soft, taste and add more seasoning if desired. Finish a soup with lemon juice, vinegar or hot sauce to brighten.Fresh chopped herbs, garlic, chili flakes or a swirl of pesto on top make the flavors pop.

Hearty additions like cooked grains or pasta, cubed tofu, roasted chickpeas or tempeh increase protein and make the meal more substantial. Blending part of the soup makes a creamy texture. Swirl in coconut milk or cream for luxury.

Get creative with soup and stew variations. Try:

- Minestrone - kidney beans, chickpeas, vegetables, macaroni, pesto
- Lentil and tomato - carrots, celery, garlic, cumin, ginger
- Curried pumpkin or sweet potato - coconut milk, curry paste, chickpeas
- Tortilla soup - black beans, corn, zucchini, chili powder, avocado
- Ramen - mushrooms, spinach, carrots, miso paste, noodles
- Chili - pinto beans, onion, peppers, mushrooms, chili powder

Soups and stews make inexpensive, hearty meals to make ahead. Cook a big batch and freeze portions for grab-and-go lunches and dinners later. They improve in flavor as leftovers too.

With endless possible combinations, soups and stews will become staples in your plant-based routine. They freeze perfectly for meal prepping or enjoying the flavors develop over days. Get creative with vegetables, beans, aromatics and spices!

Sandwiches and wraps

Sandwiches and wraps make quick, hearty plant-based meals and snacks any time of day. Stuffed with protein-packed fillings and crunchy veggies between slices of bread or wrapped in a tortilla, they are endlessly customizable. This chapter will explore delicious vegan sandwich ideas, tips for building wraps, and how to elevate your plant-powered sandwiches and wraps.

First, let's look at bread options. Sliced bread, rolls, bagels, pita and tortillas all make excellent sandwich vessels. Look for 100% whole grain varieties, or gluten-free if needed. Hearty sourdough, seeded breads and flax bread pack extra nutrition.

For great flavor and texture contrast, try mixing it up with two slices of different breads or a roll on the bottom and bread slice on top. Get creative with bread by using waffles or stuffing breads like potato rolls too.

In terms of fillings, you are limited only by your imagination. Sandwiches and wraps make great use of leftovers, so utilize roasted or grilled veggies, bean and grain dishes, hummus and more. Some other satisfying plant proteins include:

- Slices of grilled, baked or fried tofu
- Smashed chickpea or lentil salad
- Plant-based deli slices
- Bean burgers or veggie burger patties
- Nut butter and tempeh bacon
- Peanut sauce tofu or seitan

Then pile on all the fixings: avocado, sprouts, shredded lettuce and carrots, tomatoes, cucumbers, roasted peppers, mushrooms, caramelized onions, sauerkraut, pickles, etc. Condiments like mustard, olive tapenade, vegan pesto and hummus add even more flavor.

Here are some winning combos to spark sandwich inspiration:

- Chickpea salad, avocado, lettuce, tomato, onion, mustard on sprouted grain
- Tofu bacon, lettuce, tomato, avocado, vegan mayo on sourdough
- Leftover veggie burgers, grilled onions, lettuce, thousand island dressing on a bun
- Peanut butter, jam, banana slices on whole wheat bread
- Smoked tempeh, sauerkraut, tomato, spicy mustard on rye
- Veggies, hummus, sun-dried tomatoes, balsamic glaze on pita or flatbread
- Baked tofu, cucumber, bell pepper, cabbage carrot slaw on a bagel

To build a stellar wrap, lay a large tortilla flat and cover the lower third with your desired fillings, leaving the edges clear. Loosely roll up the bottom, then fold in the sides and continue tightly rolling into a wrap.

Good tortillas for wrapping are large flour, whole wheat, spinach, tomato basil or pesto. Spread hummus, tahini, vegan cream cheese or dressing inside the tortilla first. Some tasty wrap combos include:

- Curried chickpeas, brown rice, roasted cauliflower, tahini dressing
- Tofu feta, quinoa, grated carrots, spinach, hummus
- BBQ jackfruit, purple cabbage slaw, brown rice, avocado

Take sandwiches and wraps up a notch by getting creative with flavors, textures and combinations. Use cookie cutters on bread or tortillas for fun shapes. Try waffle maker presses, panini grills or a sandwich cake for party platters. The options are endless for plant-fueled handheld meals!

Buddha bowls

Buddha bowls have become a popular plant-based meal for their endless customization options and nourishing ingredients. Sometimes called plant bowls or hippie bowls, Buddha bowls feature whole grains, greens, proteins and flavorful sauces. The balanced combo of carbs, healthy fats and veggies makes Buddha bowls nutritious and satisfying.

At the base of the bowl, choose from whole grains like quinoa, brown rice, farro or millet. Whole grain bowls contribute energizing complex carbs along with fiber and B-vitamins. Alternatively, use veggie noodles like zucchini noodles or sweet potato noodles for a lighter gluten-free option.

Loading your bowl with vegetables helps boost nutrition. Spinach, kale, arugula and romaine are all excellent salad green choices. Add onions, mushrooms, bell peppers, broccoli, cauliflower or any other favorite veggies. Roasting vegetables brings out new depths of flavor.

Don't forget the plant-based protein such as lentils, chickpeas, black beans, tofu, tempeh or edamame. You can also include nuts, seeds or nut butter for plant-based fat and protein. Tofu cubes or scoops of chickpeas add hearty satisfaction.

Toppings really make the bowl according to your taste preferences. Nutritional yeast, seeds, nuts, herbs and spices are all good options. Chili flakes, sesame seeds, hemp seeds, cilantro, basil and green onions add loads of flavor.

The fun is in the sauces and dressings that tie everything together. Hummus, tahini, peanut sauce, salsa and olive tapenade offer creaminess. Pesto or chimichurri lend herbaceous notes. Nut butter or miso based dressings provide umami. Hot sauce, ponzu, teriyaki or tamari satisfy the craving for something salty and savory.

Some Buddha bowl combinations could include:

- Quinoa, kale, roasted sweet potato, baked tofu, hemp seeds, tahini dressing
- Brown rice, spinach, chickpeas, avocado, sunflower seeds, green goddess dressing
- Millet, zucchini noodles, white beans, sun-dried tomatoes, basil pesto
- Sweet potato noodles, broccoli slaw, edamame, mango, chili cashews, Thai peanut sauce

Buddha bowls make it easy to load up on whole food nutrition for lunch or dinner. They come together quickly by layering grains or noodles, sauteed or raw veggies, plant proteins and toppings of your choice. The variations are endless, so you can enjoy a new Buddha bowl creation daily!

Pasta dishes

Pasta makes for quick, budget-friendly and satisfying meals that can be adapted endlessly for the plant-based diet. With whole grain noodles, plant-based proteins, and veggies galore, pasta night will become a new favorite.

Opt for 100% whole grain pastas made from quinoa, brown rice, buckwheat or whole wheat. These provide more nutrients, protein and fiber than plain semolina pastas. Alternatively, explore pastas made from beans, lentils or chickpeas for extra plant-based protein.

Watch out for pasta sneaking in eggs or dairy. With so many varieties available now, it's easy to find plant-based noodles from gluten-free to organic to high protein. Cook pasta al dente to retain nutrients.

Sauces bring endless possibilities. Marinara is classic, but don't stop there. Creamy nut or seed based sauces, pestos, olive oil and fresh veggie combos, spicy arrabiatas and herb-filled pestos offer variety.

For a protein punch, stir in shelled edamame, crispy tofu or tempeh cubes, white beans, or lentils. Roasted veggies like eggplant, mushrooms and zucchini make hearty additions.

Some tasty pasta and sauce combinations include:

- Tomato basil - Marinara, fresh tomatoes, basil, garlic
- Primavera - Mixed vegetables, olive oil, lemon juice, parsley
- Pesto - Basil, pine nuts, olive oil, garlic, lemon
- Alfredo - Cashew cream, nutritional yeast, garlic, lemon

- Puttanesca - Olives, capers, tomato sauce, chili flakes
- Arrabiata - Spicy tomato sauce, chili peppers, garlic
- Bolognese - Lentils, walnuts, mushrooms, tomatoes, herbs
- Carbonara - Tofu, coconut bacon, nutritional yeast, sauce
- Cacio e pepe - Cauliflower, ground pepper, nutritional yeast

Turn leftovers into pasta casseroles or soup. Chill cooked pasta separately from sauce, then combine and bake with cheese or breadcrumbs. Toss with veggies and broth for pasta fagioli soup.

Make the most of seasonal produce like sundried tomatoes, artichokes, roasted pumpkin or butternut squash. Basil, tomatoes and zucchini star in summer. Hearty mushrooms and kale shine in cooler months.

If pressed for time, homemade sauces can often be swapped with quality jarred sauces. Add sautéed veggies, fresh herbs and plant proteins to elevate store-bought sauce.

Some helpful tips for perfect pasta:

- Salt cooking water well to infuse flavor
- Reserve starchy pasta water to thin sauces
- Cook veggies just until tender before adding sauce
- Simmer sauce briefly to meld flavors
- Finish with fresh herbs, lemon juice or nutritional yeast

Pasta bakes well for meal prep. Assemble uncooked pasta, sauce and mix-ins in a baking dish, then cover and bake when ready to eat. Customize pasta bakes with themes like eggplant parm, pesto lasagna or mac and cheese.

Healthy, satisfying and budget-friendly, whole grain pasta makes the perfect canvas for exploring plant-based creativity. It's easy to whip up a nutritious pasta dinner on a weeknight or dress it up for company. Mangia!

CHAPTER 6

NOURISHING DINNERS

Bean dishes

Beans are one of the most versatile, nutritious staples for plant-based cooking. Full of fiber, protein, and essential vitamins and minerals, beans can be transformed into appetizers, main dishes, sides, soups, salads, and more. This chapter will overview simple ways to cook beans from scratch, how to use canned beans, and delicious recipes to incorporate beans into well-rounded vegan and vegetarian meals.

Dried beans are inexpensive, shelf-stable, and environmentally sustainable. Cooking your own allows you to control sodium content. Most beans only require soaking, simmering, and seasonings to become tender and flavorful.

Quick-soak methods reduce prep time. Boil beans for 2 minutes, then let sit in the water 1 hour. Otherwise, soak 8 hours or overnight, then drain and rinse. Simmer in fresh water until soft, usually 1-2 hours. Add aromatics like onions, garlic, herbs and spices for extra flavor.

Canned beans offer convenience, but may have added salt and less nutrition. Rinse and drain them before using to remove excess sodium. Canned beans are pre-cooked – simply heat and add seasonings. Opt for low-sodium or no-salt-added varieties when possible.

Beans pair deliciously with grains, veggies, greens, nuts and seeds. They provide texture and nutrition to salads, bowls, tacos, stews, soups, pastas, casseroles and more. Mix and match different beans and legumes. Here are some easy plant-based recipes:

- Black bean burritos with rice, salsa, guacamole
- White bean and kale soup with garlic and rosemary
- Three bean chili with corn, zucchini and peppers

- Edamame and chickpea Buddha bowl with quinoa
- Lentil sloppy joes with mushrooms and caramelized onions
- Baked beans with diced sweet potatoes and smoked paprika
- Hummus and bean dip platter with fresh veggie sticks
- Pinto bean and walnut taco "meat" in lettuce wraps
- Curried red lentil dal with wilted spinach
- White bean alfredo sauce with pasta and roasted broccoli
- Black eyed peas and collard greens stew
- Baked bean and tempeh bacon tacos with slaw
- Red beans and rice with mirepoix and cajun seasoning
- Mixed bean and barley soup with kale pesto swirl
- Edamame avocado salad with vinaigrette and sunflower seeds

The possibilities are endless when cooking with beans! They add nutrition, heartiness, and fiber to plant-forward dishes. Making a batch of cooked beans to have on hand saves time too.

Get creative with spices, marinades, sauces and globally inspired bean recipes. Added extras like nuts, seeds and greens amp up flavors and textures even more. Give beans a starring role in your plant-based meal planning. They are affordable, satisfying and brimming with goodness.

Veggie burgers

Veggie burgers are a plant-based staple, satisfying the craving for a hearty, flavorful sandwich with an easy-to-eat handheld option. Luckily, it's simple to whip up homemade veggie burgers that are far superior to frozen varieties. With the right ingredients, seasonings and binders, you can make your plant-based burgers packed with good-for-you ingredients.

When making veggie burger patties, chopped vegetables provide moisture and texture. Good options are mushrooms, carrots, beans, sweet potatoes, beets or zucchini. Finely chop or pulse in a food processor. You want the veggies grated finely to help bind the burgers.

Beans or lentils add protein and bulk to help hold the patties together. Kidney beans, black beans, chickpeas or red lentils work well. Cooked quinoa or oats also provide binding power.

For additional moisture and binding action, include a flax egg (1 Tbsp ground flax + 3 Tbsp water). Other binders like egg replacer, vital wheat gluten, or chia seeds help adherence too.

Whole grain breadcrumbs, crushed crackers or oats give body that holds the patty together on the grill or pan. Rolled oats work well.

To boost flavor, incorporate spices, sauces and herbs like cumin, garlic powder, onion powder, smoked paprika, parsley, basil, ketchup or tamari. Ketchup and tomato paste help mimic the flavor of traditional beef burgers.

Nutritional yeast adds savory, cheesy notes while providing B-vitamins. Salt, pepper and vinegar or lemon juice contribute seasoning. Mustard, relish, barbecue or hot sauce also enhance flavor.

Good fats lend juiciness to the patties on the grill. Canola oil, olive oil, mashed avocado, nut butter or soaked nuts increase richness. But don't overdo it, excessive oil causes falling apart.

Keeping veggie burger patties together on the grill takes a few tricks. Refrigerate the patties for at least 30 minutes before grilling, this helps firm up the mixture. Use parchment paper under patties if sticking. Grill on medium heat, resisting urge to move them until ready to flip.

Serve plant-based burgers in a whole grain bun with all your favorite toppings and condiments like lettuce, tomato, onion, pickles, ketchup, mustard, vegan mayo or cheese. Baked sweet potato fries on the side complete the meal.

With the right blend of vegetables, starches, binders and flavorings, you can create tasty homemade veggie burgers to enjoy again and again. Experiment until you find your perfect plant-based burger.

Vegetable curries

Vegetable curries are a delicious way to pack more plants into your diet and discover new flavors. The combination of aromatic spices, protein-rich legumes, tender produce and creamy coconut milk is irresistible. Curries are easy to make plant-based.

Curry describes dishes originating from Southern Asia that blend complex spice blends like ginger, coriander, cumin, turmeric, cinnamon, cardamom, chili peppers, fenugreek and more. Making your own curry paste from these spices is simple.

Start by sautéing a minced onion, garlic, fresh ginger and any other aromatics to build a flavor base. Cook briefly until soft and fragrant. Stir in spices and cook another minute or two to release their oils. Finally, add a can of coconut milk and chopped vegetables.

Potatoes, cauliflower, peas, carrots, bell peppers and green beans all work beautifully in curries. Chop denser veggies small so they cook through. Cherry tomatoes, spinach and tender greens can be added near the end.

Chickpeas, lentils or beans provide protein, fiber and body. Cubed extra firm tofu also pairs perfectly with curries. Add these along with denser vegetables so they have time to soak up flavors.

Simmer the vegetable curry 15-20 minutes until veggies are fork tender. If the sauce reduces too much, splash in more coconut milk or non-dairy milk. Taste and adjust seasoning as needed.

Finish the curry with a squeeze of lime juice, a sprinkle of cilantro or chopped nuts. Serve atop brown rice, quinoa or whole grain flatbread. A cooling yogurt raita balances the heat.

Here are some tasty vegetable curry flavor ideas:

- Coconut curried pumpkin or sweet potato with chickpeas and spinach
- Thai red curry with bamboo shoots, peppers and basil
- Indian chickpea curry with cauliflower, peas and tomatoes
- Malaysian laksa with tofu, cabbage, sprouts and ginger
- Japanese curry with kabocha squash, edamame and carrots
- West African peanut stew with sweet potatoes, greens and beans

Improvising curries is easy once your pantry is stocked with versatile spice staples. Start with aromatics, main veggies, protein source, spices and coconut milk. Simmer until cooked through and voila - weekday dinner ready in under an hour.

Roasting vegetables before adding them to curry deepens the flavors. Blending the sauce makes it extra creamy. Serve over grains or stuff into a pita or wraps for grab and go lunches. Leftovers keep well for a few days.

Embrace eating the rainbow by trying produce you rarely use. Exploring new vegetables and global flavors expands the palate. Curries provide a passport for tastebud travel from India to Thailand, Japan and beyond!

With dozens of possible vegetable, protein and spice combinations, curries will never get boring. Stock your pantry with curry paste and coconut milk so you can whip up nourishing, fragrant plant-based cuisine anytime.

Stir fries

Stir frying is a quick, healthy cooking technique that's perfect for weeknight plant-based dinners. Fresh vegetables and plant proteins get a flash sauté in a hot wok or skillet to create colorful, flavorful dishes. Endlessly adaptable, stir fries make it easy to use up fridge veggies and customize flavors. This chapter will explore the basics of stir frying, key ingredients, sauces and seasonings, and some simple vegan stir fry recipes to try at home.

A stir fry comes together in minutes by cutting ingredients into uniform pieces and stir frying over high heat. The intense heat helps caramelize veggies and seal in flavor. A wok or large nonstick skillet work best to allow quick tossing of ingredients.

Start with an aromatic base. Mince garlic and ginger and optionally chilies, shallots or lemongrass. Cook briefly in oil to release fragrance before adding veggies. Go for colorful combos – broccoli, bell peppers, snap peas, mushrooms, bok choy, green beans, etc.

Slice firmer veggies thinner to cook quickly. Add tender greens like spinach at the end. Marinate tofu or tempeh to amp up protein. Cook in batches if needed to avoid crowding the pan.

Toss constantly using a spatula or wok tool to prevent burning. A small amount of broth, water, coconut milk or wine adds steam for a sauce that clings nicely to ingredients.

Finish with a sauce based on your flavors – soy, oyster or hoisin sauce, peanut or almond butter, citrus juice, sesame oil, rice vinegar, sriracha, etc. Toasted sesame seeds, scallions and cilantro add garnish.

Here are some easy plant-based stir fry ideas:

- Tofu and bok choy in garlic ginger sauce
- Asparagus and shiitake mushrooms with teriyaki
- Broccoli and carrots in spicy chili garlic sauce
- Tempeh, snap peas and water chestnuts in hoisin
- Seitan, bell peppers and pineapple in sweet chili sauce
- Eggplant, basil and green beans in soy ginger glaze
- Cauliflower fried rice with peas, carrots and cashews
- Zucchini noodles, kale and hemp hearts in almond butter sauce
- Curried chickpeas, potatoes and spinach with coconut milk

- Tofu, cabbage, edamame and mushrooms in sesame soy

- Broccoli, carrots, peppers and mung beans with Thai peanut sauce

- Black bean, corn and red pepper fajita stir fry

Amp up nutrition with brown rice, quinoa or soba noodles on the side or tossed in. Peanuts, cashews or fresh herbs add extra flavor. Clear the fridge out by stir frying leftover roasted veggies and grains.

With an array of sauces and seasonings, the possibilities are endless for improvising plant-based stir fries. They come together in a flash, making them perfect fast, healthy weeknight dinners. Just chop, toss, and dinner is served!

Casseroles and bakes

There's something so comforting about cozying up to a warm, hearty casserole or baked dish. Luckily, it's easy to veganize all your favorite casseroles by using plant-based proteins, non-dairy milks, and loads of veggies. With a few simple substitutions, you can still enjoy the nostalgic flavors of these baked one-dish meals.

At the base of casseroles, use either whole grains or pasta/noodles. Brown rice, quinoa, barley, farro and whole wheat pasta or noodles hold up well. For gluten-free options, try chickpea pasta or zucchini noodles.

Chopped vegetables add nutrition, texture and flavor. Good choices are peppers, onions, carrots, spinach, broccoli, cauliflower, sweet potatoes, zucchini or eggplant. Mushrooms lend a meaty, umami quality. Roast veggies first to bring out sweetness.

For creamy casseroles, blend silken tofu, vegan cream cheese or soaked raw cashews into the sauce or gravy base. Unsweetened non-dairy milk thickens and provides richness when blended with flour or starch.

Incorporate beans or lentils for a protein boost, such as kidney beans, chickpeas, black beans and green or brown lentils. Tofu, tempeh, seitan or crumbles also work.

Season with garlic, onion, nutritional yeast, white miso, or tamari for savory depth. Herbs like basil, oregano, thyme and parsley keep it fresh. Lemon juice brightens flavors.

For binding and overall thickness, use breadcrumbs, oat flour or mashed potatoes. A small amount of all-purpose flour helps thicken and hold casseroles together.

Top with crunchy elements before baking such as crispy panko breadcrumbs, toasted nuts or seeds, crushed tortilla chips or oven-roasted chickpeas. This adds nice contrast.

Some winning plant-based casserole recipes to try include:

- Veggie Pot Pie with chickpeas, carrots, peas and mushrooms in a creamy veggie gravy.
- Eggplant Parmesan with layers of breaded eggplant, tomato sauce and non-dairy mozzarella cheese.
- Bean Enchiladas with black beans, corn, peppers, onions wrapped in tortillas and smothered in enchilada sauce and avocado.
- Mac and Cheese Casserole made with cauliflower alfredo sauce and nut-based cheese.
- Chili Frito Pie using veggie chili over corn chips and a mashed avocado topping.
- Lentil Shepherd's Pie topped with creamy mashed potatoes.

If you want a comforting one-dish meal that's still wholesome, try a new plant-based casserole or bake. With clever ingredient swaps, you can continue enjoying these cozy classics.

Plant-based pizza

Pizza night can still be a weekly ritual with endless plant-based possibilities for healthy homemade pies. Using veggie-packed toppings, plant-based cheese and whole grain crusts makes pizza night both fun and nutritious.

Start with a pre-made whole grain thin crust, a ready-to-go pizza dough, or try making your own using whole wheat flour. Hand tossing dough is fun and impresses guests. Even just pizza sauce and veggies on a flatbread or tortilla can hit the spot.

Go beyond marinara with creative sauces like hummus, nut-based pesto or white bean spreads as the base. Roasted garlic, spinach or sun-dried tomatoes blended into sauce boosts nutrition.

Pile on the veggies generously—the more the better! Fresh or roasted vegetables add nutrients, texture and color. Mushrooms, peppers, onions, tomatoes, spinach, broccoli, zucchini, eggplant and olives are classic pizza toppings.

Try unique plant-based proteins like marinated artichoke hearts, sun-dried tomatoes and roasted chickpeas in addition to veggie meats. Sprinkle hemp or pumpkin seeds over top for a nutritious crunch.

The plant-based cheese options now available mean you don't have to miss out on gooey, melty cheese. Brands like Daiya, Follow Your Heart and Miyoko's offer shreds, slices and blocks in mozzarella, cheddar and pepper jack styles.

Or make your own cashew cheese sauce to drizzle over the pizza. Soak raw cashews, then blend with nutritional yeast, lemon juice, garlic and seasonings for a tangy "cheese." Sprinkle extra nutritional yeast over any dairy-free cheese for added flavor.

Some fun plant-based pizza combinations to try:

- Pesto, tomatoes, artichokes, spinach
- Hummus, roasted veggies, sun-dried tomatoes
- Cashew cream sauce, caramelized onions, mushrooms
- Marinara, vegan sausage, red onion, bell pepper
- Olive tapenade, roasted chickpeas, olives, arugula

Get creative with globally inspired pizzas too like tandoori roasted cauliflower or Thai peanut sauce. Make mini individual veggie pizzas for parties. Pizza also reheats well for quick leftovers.

Turn pizza making interactive with build your own pizza stations. Set out individual crusts and let guests personalize with sauces, cheeses and toppings of choice. It's a fun activity for weeknights or get-togethers.

Making homemade pizza is easier than you think. Start with a pre-made crust to save time. Load up the veggies and plant-based proteins for a filling meal. Customize pies to please all palates by offering a DIY toppings bar.

Pizza the plant-based way maximizes nutrition and endless creativity. Gather friends or family weekly and take turns concocting veggie-loaded signature pizzas. Get the kids involved in inventing fun new flavor combos. Plant-based pizza night delivers endless possibilities!

CHAPTER 7
SAVORY SNACKS AND APPETIZERS

Dips and spreads

Dips and spreads are versatile plant-powered appetizers and snacks. Bean dips, nut butters, tapenades, pestos and more are easy to whip up and full of nutrition. This chapter will explore flavourful vegan dips, creative ways to use them, tips for upgrading store-bought options, and simple homemade spreads that come together quickly.

Hummus is a dip staple that can be blended up quickly from canned or cooked chickpeas, tahini, lemon, garlic and olive oil. Try mix-ins like roasted red peppers, sun-dried tomatoes, roasted garlic or greens. Pair with pita chips or fresh vegetables.

White bean dip has a similar creamy texture. Blend cooked white beans with olive oil, garlic and herbs like rosemary, then season to taste. Great as a sandwich spread too. For creaminess without the fat, use beans, silken tofu or vegan yogurt in dips.

Baba ghanoush, made from roasted eggplant and tahini, has a rich smoky flavor. Black bean dip is protein-packed and fiber-rich. And guacamole is a quick mash of avocado, onion, tomato, lime and cilantro.

Tapenades made from olives, artichokes or roasted red peppers make bold, briny dips. Pulse nuts like walnuts or almonds into nut butters with olive oil and salt for instant dips.

Vegan pesto is easy to make from basil, olive oil, nuts, garlic and lemon. Spinach or kale can be swapped for the basil. Drizzle on flatbreads or use as a sandwich spread.

Roasting vegetables and blending into dips adds depth of flavor. Try roasting cauliflower, carrots, beets or squash to blend into dips.

For store-bought varieties, check labels to avoid hidden animal products in packaged dips and spreads. Look for vegan specialty brands or hummus and guacamole made fresh in stores.

To upgrade store-bought dips:

- Add a squeeze of lemon or lime juice for a brightness
- Extra garlic, salt and pepper boosts flavor
- Stir in chopped herbs like cilantro, dill, or chives
- Swirl in olive oil or tahini for creaminess
- Fold in diced tomatoes or chopped roasted red peppers

Homemade nut-based cheeses are great dairy-free dips too. Blend soaked nuts like cashews, macadamia or almonds into a creamy "cheese" base, then add herbs, spices or vegetables to create spreads with the flavors you love.

Get creative with combinations of beans, nut butters, oils, fresh herbs and roasted veggies. Play with global flavors – curry powder, harissa, za'atar, etc. – to make culturally inspired dips.

Serving ideas:

- Roasted eggplant dip with grilled flatbread wedges
- Chickpea avocado dip with baked tortilla chips
- White bean rosemary spread on potato crisps
- Beet hummus with celery and carrot sticks
- Sun-dried tomato pesto crostini
- Baba ghanoush with za'atar pita chips
- Smashed peas and mint dip with rice crackers

With a well-stocked pantry, plant-based dips and spreads come together in minutes. Beans, nut butters, oils, herbs and spices are great building blocks. Serve with veggie sticks, crackers, breads or tortilla chips for quick, nutritious snacks and appetizers.

Roasted chickpeas

Crispy, crunchy roasted chickpeas make for the perfect plant-based snack or salad topper. Roasting brings out their natural sweetness and creates an irresistibly poppable texture. With just a few seasonings, chickpeas transform into a moreish snack you can feel good about munching anytime.

Chickpeas are nutritionally well-rounded, providing fiber, protein, iron, magnesium, potassium and folate. When roasted, the starch on the outer skin of the chickpea crystallizes, creating delicious crunch. The inside stays creamy and tender.

Prepping the chickpeas for roasting is simple. Drain and rinse 1-2 cans of chickpeas. Dry them thoroughly using paper towels or a salad spinner until no moisture remains on the surface. This helps them get crispy.

Toss the chickpeas with just enough oil to lightly coat - usually 1-2 tablespoons per can. Olive oil or avocado oil work well since they have high smoke points. This allows the natural flavors to shine through.

Season the oiled chickpeas generously with your choice of spices and dried herbs. Options like smoked paprika, garlic powder, onion powder, ground cumin, chili powder, za'atar and Italian seasoning all create dynamic flavor. Sea salt brings out chickpeas' natural sweetness.

Spread seasoned chickpeas in a single layer on a parchment lined baking sheet. Roast at 400oF for 35-45 minutes, tossing once halfway through. They are ready when browned and shrunken, making hollow sounds when tapped.

Beyond basic roasted chickpeas, there are many flavor variations to try:

- Chili Lime Chickpeas - Toss coated chickpeas with lime zest, chili powder, cumin and cayenne.

- Curry Coconut Chickpeas - Coat with coconut oil and curry powder. Finish with lime juice and cilantro.

- Pizza Chickpeas - Season with oregano, garlic, onion powder, smoked paprika and nutritional yeast.

- Cinnamon Sugar Chickpeas - Toss in cinnamon and brown sugar for a sweet snack.

- Ranch Chickpeas - Use dried parsley, dill, garlic powder, onion powder and black pepper.

For salads, bowls or snacks, roasted chickpeas provide satisfying crunch and nutrition. Store any extras in an airtight container for up to 1 week. Whip up a batch or two each week for grab-and-go plant-based protein. With endless seasoning options, you'll never get bored with these craveably crisp and delicious roasted chickpeas.

Vegetable fritters

Vegetable fritters are a fun and tasty way to sneak more plants into your diet. Grate or finely chop produce, bind with chickpea flour or crumbs, and pan fry for crispy, nutrient-packed snacks or meals. The possibilities are endless!

Almost any vegetable can be turned into fritter form. Harder produce like carrots, sweet potatoes, beets and parsnips grate well raw. Softer veggies like zucchini, spinach and kale should be squeezed of excess moisture before mixing.

Grating on the small holes of a box grater or pulsing in a food processor yields finely shredded texture best for fritters. Drain any excess liquid released. You want the veggie mixture as dry as possible.

Chickpea flour acts as a binder when mixed with the shredded vegetables, helping hold the fritters together when cooked. Flax or chia seeds blended with water perform similarly.

Add spices like cumin, paprika, garlic, parsley or chili flakes to boost flavor. Chopped nuts or seeds add healthy fats and crunch. Nutritional yeast, tahini or hummus make great emulsifiers too.

Let the vegetable mixture sit 5-10 minutes after mixing to let binders act. Then form into patties by hand, pressing to pack together. Refrigerate 20-30 minutes if time allows to set up further.

Pan fry the patties in a thin layer of oil over medium heat until crispy and browned on both sides, about 4-5 minutes per side. Drain on paper towels.

Some tasty veggie fritter combinations include:

- Carrot-Ginger - Shredded carrots, parsley, ginger, garlic, chickpea flour
- Zucchini-Basil - Shredded zucchini, basil, garlic, almond flour
- Beet-Walnut - Shredded beets, walnuts, lemon zest, chia seeds
- Broccoli-Cheddar - Finely chopped broccoli, nutritional yeast, chickpea flour
- Spinach-Artichoke - Chopped spinach, artichokes, breadcrumbs, flax eggs
- Tex Mex - Shredded potatoes, corn, cumin, paprika, pepper jack cheese

Vegetable fritters make a complete meal served with greens or a grain like quinoa. For easy hors d'oeuvres, cut fritters into bite-sized pieces. They also pair well with yogurt or chutney dips.

Meal prep batches by forming uncooked fritter patties, placing them on a sheet pan lined with parchment and freezing. Once frozen, transfer to a ziplock bag. Pull out only what you need to pan fry each day.

Let kids create their own fun shaped fritters using cookie cutters. Try broccoli trees, carrot stars, and zucchini hearts for more whimsy. Creative shapes and combinations will make veggie fritters a favorite.

Vegetable fritters are a stellar way to use up produce before it goes bad. You can substitute almost any veggie into basic fritter recipes. Embrace the chance to experiment with unfamiliar vegetables too!

Stuffed mushrooms

Stuffed mushrooms are a perfect plant-based party appetizer or weeknight side. They sound fancy, but are easy to whip up and endlessly adaptable. Mini mushroom caps are filled with savory vegan ingredients, then roasted or baked until tender. This chapter explores different stuffing combinations, how to prepare and cook stuffed mushrooms, and recipes to inspire your plant-powered mushroom endeavors.

Button, cremini or portobello mushrooms all work beautifully stuffed. Opt for mushrooms with caps at least 2 inches wide for easier filling. Clean the mushrooms and remove stems, reserving for other uses like stocks or sautéing.

To enhance flavor, brush the mushroom caps lightly with olive oil or vegan butter and season with salt and pepper before filling. For fillings, simply mix crumbled tofu, vegan cheese, nuts, lentils or veggies with seasonings and binders until combined.

Some flavorful plant-based stuffed mushroom filling ideas include:

- Breadcrumbs, walnuts, garlic, lemon zest, herbs
- Roasted garlic, spinach, sun-dried tomatoes, vegan feta
- Corn, black beans, cilantro, cumin, lime juice
- Pecans, vegan pesto, diced artichokes, breadcrumbs
- Diced apple, cranberries, thyme, toasted oats
- Lentils, carrots, parsley, smoked paprika, almonds
- Tofu, garlic, nutritional yeast, salt, pepper

- Mixed shredded veggies, hummus, cumin, tahini
- Chopped kale, pinto beans, onion, chili powder
- Broccoli, cashews, mustard, panko breadcrumbs

Pack the filling lightly into the mushroom caps, mounding slightly. Bake at 375F for 15-20 minutes until filling is set and mushrooms tender. Baking let's the juices meld into the filling.

For a quick cook method, brush caps with oil, fill, then sauté in batches over medium-high heat until lightly browned. Cook just 2-4 minutes per side. The filling will soften as the mushrooms cook.

Garnish stuffed mushrooms with extra herbs, a spritz of lemon, or vegan parmesan. Accompany them with dipping sauce like vegan ranch, marinara or roasted red pepper sauce.

Serve stuffed mushrooms as passed hors d'oeuvres, on a platter at parties, or alongside salads and grain bowls. They make great snacks, meatless meals, or holiday sides.

Some full stuffed mushroom recipe ideas include:

- Garlic lemon oyster mushrooms stuffed with basil pine nut pesto
- Portobellos with sun-dried tomato quinoa filling and balsamic glaze
- Creminis filled with smoked almond veggie crust and roasted red pepper drizzle
- Mixed wild mushrooms with pecan shallot breadcrumb stuffing
- Buttons filled with spinach, artichoke and macadamia "cheese"

Infuse your stuffed mushrooms with global flavors – curries, Mediterranean herbs, Latin American spices, etc. Play with textures by mixing in nuts, seeds, whole grains and crunchy breadcrumbs.

Stuffed mushrooms are elegant yet easy to prepare in advance for parties or gatherings. They showcase how flavorful and satisfying plant-based cooking can be. Let your creativity run wild with all the possible stuffed mushroom variations!

Veggie skewers

Veggie skewers make an easy plant-based option for grilling or roasting. Threading vegetables and plant proteins onto skewers results in tasty lightly charred flavors. The skewer presentation also makes them ideal for parties and barbecues.

Almost any vegetable can be skewered after cutting into bite-sized pieces. Try combinations like tomatoes, zucchini, potatoes, bell peppers, mushrooms, pearl onions, corn, pineapple, peach, eggplant or plantain. Soak woody vegetables like potatoes in water briefly to prevent burning.

Small whole vegetables also work well, like cherry tomatoes, baby potatoes, shallots or Brussels sprouts. For corn, break ears into 2-3 sections to skewer. Cut tofu, tempeh, seitan or plant meats into cubes for added protein.

Wooden or metal skewers both work fine, just remember to soak wooden skewers in water for 30 minutes first to prevent burning. Line a sheet pan with parchment paper or foil and lightly coat with oil before placing assembled skewers to prevent sticking.

When it comes to seasoning, get creative with sauces, glazes, spices and herbs. A good basic approach is coating with olive oil first, then sprinkling on desired seasonings. Herbs, spices, salt, pepper, onion powder, garlic powder, smoked paprika and chili powder are all safe bets.

For flavorful sauces and glazes, try:

- Peanut sauce
- Teriyaki
- Pesto
- Chimichurri

- Balsamic glaze
- Barbecue sauce
- Thai chili sauce
- Ponzu
- Harissa or sriracha

Brush glazes on during last 5 minutes of cooking to avoid burning.

Grill skewers over medium heat for 12-15 minutes, turning occasionally until vegetables are tender with char marks. If roasting, bake at 425°F for 18-22 minutes.

Serve veggie skewers on their own or over greens or grains like couscous, quinoa, rice or pasta salad. They make the perfect plant-based addition to summer grilling. Get creative with combinations and flavors.

Harber Curry

CHAPTER 8
DELECTABLE DESSERTS

Cookies

Cookies satisfy sweet cravings and make the perfect plant-based treat. With smart swaps for eggs, butter and milk, it's easy to veganize any cookie recipe. Creative add-ins like nuts, seeds, dried fruit and chocolate make for endless flavor possibilities.

To replace eggs, flax eggs made from ground flaxseed and water work beautifully in cookies. The ground chia seeds or banana mashed with water also substitute well. For each egg in a recipe, use 1 tablespoon ground flax or chia whisked with 3 tablespoons water. Let thicken 5 minutes before baking.

Non-hydrogenated vegetable shortening, coconut oil or vegan butter stand in for regular butter or shortening. Measure the same amount as the original recipe calls for. The consistency may slightly differ from traditional butter, but will bake similarly.

Swap dairy milk with any non-dairy milk like almond, soy, oat or coconut. For thicker cookie dough, coconut milk works especially well. Use the same amount of plant milk as cow milk required.

With the egg and dairy substitutions, you're set to bake up any cookie recipe plant-based. Get creative with mix-in additions to dress up basic dough.

Rich chocolate chunks, cacao nibs, peanut butter chips, nuts like walnuts or pecans, shredded coconut, oats, espresso powder, citrus zest, dried cranberries or cherries all make fabulous cookie add-ins.

Spices like cinnamon, ginger, nutmeg, cloves and cardamom add warmth and dimension of flavor. Vanilla and almond extracts infuse cookies with delicious aroma.

Some festive plant-based cookie flavor ideas include:

- Chocolate chip - Vegan chocolate chunks / nuts
- Oatmeal raisin - Vegan butter, oats, raisins, cinnamon
- Peanut butter - Vegan butter, peanut butter, chocolate
- Mexican wedding cookies - Walnuts, coconut, cinnamon
- Gingerbread - Molasses, ginger, cinnamon, allspice
- Pistachio thumbprints - Pistachios, jam filling
- Spice cookies - Warm spices, vegan butter, vanilla
- Cranberry orange - Dried cranberries, orange zest

Get the kids involved in making fun shaped cookies using cookie cutters. Set up a decorating station with sprinkles and icing for let creativity run wild.

Cookies keep well at room temperature in airtight containers for several days. Freeze dough logs before baking and slice off portions whenever fresh cookies are desired.

You'll feel good serving nourishing plant-based cookies made without dairy or eggs. With some simple ingredient tweaks, classic cookies can be part of a healthy diet - in moderation, of course!

Brownies

Fudgy, chocolatey brownies are a beloved dessert that can certainly be enjoyed on a plant-based diet. With the right ingredients and baking tips, vegan brownies can be just as decadent and delicious as any traditional recipe. This chapter will explore how to bake indulgent vegan brownies, egg and dairy substitutes, add-ins, frostings and serving ideas.

A basic brownie recipe calls for eggs and butter. To adapt for vegan diets, those ingredients need plant-based swaps. Silken tofu blends into a smooth batter that bakes up fudgy. Applesauce also substitutes well for eggs. Dairy-free butter or oil is an easy swap.

Flax eggs provide binding power too. Whisk 1 tablespoon ground flaxseed with 2.5 tablespoons water and let thicken. Swapping up the flour can increase nutrition. Try whole wheat or buckwheat flour blended with cocoa powder and spices.

In terms of cocoa powder, aim for quality over quantity. Deep, dark cocoa provides plenty of chocolate impact without overpowering the other flavors. Too much cocoa can leave brownies dry. Fold in chocolate chips or chunks for bonus decadence.

Some other delicious vegan brownie mix-ins include:

- Toasted nuts like walnuts or pecans
- Coffee or espresso powder
- Raspberries, cherries or dried fruit
- Peanut butter or other nut butters
- Shredded coconut
- Crumbled cookies or cereal
- Vegan marshmallows
- Maple syrup or cinnamon for a mocha flavor

Grease the baking pan well and evenly so the brownies release easily. Glass pans tend to bake more evenly than metal. Check for doneness early to avoid overbaking. The edges should look set, and a toothpick should come out with just a few crumbs.

Let brownies cool completely before cutting for clean slices. Dust with powdered sugar or cocoa powder, or top with chocolate ganache, caramel, fruit sauce or vegan ice cream. Sandwich brownies together with frostings.

Here are some delicious vegan brownie variations to try:

- Classic Fudgy Chocolate Brownies

- Walnut Cocoa Brownies with Chocolate Glaze
- Mexican Chocolate Brownies with cinnamon, chili powder and cayenne
- Peanut Butter Swirl Brownies with peanut butter filling
- Raspberry Cheesecake Brownies with vegan cheesecake swirl
- Coffee Toffee Crunch Brownies with almonds and sea salt
- Black Forest Brownies with cherries and coconut whipped cream
- Mint Chocolate Chip Brownies with vegan chocolate chips
- Blondies with peanut butter, chocolate chips and walnuts

With some simple substitutions and mix-ins, brownies can be prepared vegan with ease. Let the chocolatey aroma lure in a crowd to enjoy a tray of your new signature vegan brownies. They are sure to be a delicious hit!

Fruit crisps

Fruit crisps are the perfect simple, wholesome plant-based dessert. Layer fresh seasonal fruit with an oat crumble topping and bake until bubbly and golden. The combination of juicy fruit and crunchy streusel is sure to satisfy any sweet tooth.

When making a fruit crisp, let the produce be the star. Use ripe, in-season fruits at their flavor peak. Good options are stone fruits like peaches, nectarines, plums, cherries, apricots or berries like strawberries, blueberries, blackberries, raspberries. Mix up fruits for more complexity.

Slice large fruits into 1/2 inch chunks or slices. For citrus fruits like oranges or grapefruit, slice into rounds and remove any pits or seeds. Leave smaller fruits like berries whole. Toss cut fruit with just a bit of flour or starch to help thicken juices.

For the topping, combine rolled or old-fashioned oats with nuts, seeds, flour, spices, salt and just enough melted plant-based butter or oil to bind. Chopped almonds, pecans or walnuts add crunch and richness. Coconut oil or vegan butter lend buttery flavor.

Spices like cinnamon, cardamom, ginger or nutmeg complement most fruits. A small amount of sugar - brown, coconut or maple - boosts sweetness and caramelization, but let the fruit provide most of the sweetness needed.

Layer fruit into a baking dish, arrange topping evenly over fruit. Bake at 350°F for 35-45 minutes until fruit is tender and topping is browned and crispy. Serve warm with non-dairy ice cream or yogurt.

Some tasty fruit crisp combinations include:

Cherry Amaretto Crisp - Use pitted cherries and almond extract in topping. Include citrus zest for brightness.

Spiced Pear Crisp - Combine pears and apple with cinnamon, cardamom, cloves and ginger. Toast pecans into streusel.

Triple Berry Crisp - Use equal amounts of raspberries, blueberries and strawberries for berry explosion. Add lemon zest.

Peach & Plum Crisp - Offset sweet peaches with tart plums. Add oat and almond crumble.

Apple Brown Butter Crisp - Saute apples in browned vegan butter first for depth.

With the right fruit choices and creative crumble toppings, fruit crisps are simple to veganize. The preparation is easy but results in a decadent treat full of cozy, nostalgic flavor. It's a comfort food dessert that highlights nature's bounty.

Pies

Nothing satisfies a sweet tooth like a hearty slice of homemade pie. With plant-based ingredients, it's easy to veganize this comforting classic. Fruit and nut pies make natural options, while pumpkin, pecan and chocolate shine with non-dairy milks and egg replacers.

The crust sets the foundation. Opt for plant-based varieties from brands like Wholly Wholesome or Mrs. Smith's, or make your own using coconut oil or vegan butter with whole wheat flour. Chill dough thoroughly before rolling for easy handling.

Blind bake empty pie crusts 5 minutes before filling. For a cookie crumb crust, press finely ground cookies or graham crackers into the pan. Chia seeds or flax eggs bind fruit fillings.

Apples, berries, peaches, pineapple and other fruits transform into luscious pies. Cook fruit with sugar and cornstarch to thicken. Spices like cinnamon or nutmeg add warmth. Allow cooked fillings to cool fully before adding to the crust.

Nuts also make tasty pie fillings. Toast pecans, walnuts or almonds then process into a coarse meal. Add maple syrup, coconut sugar or dates to bind. A touch of non-dairy milk or liqueur amps up flavor.

For cream pies, blend silken tofu, coconut cream or cashews with plant milk, sugar and extracts. Thicken with cornstarch or tapioca starch. Chill thoroughly once added to the pie shell. Top with whipped coconut cream.

Turn up the volume on pumpkin pie with bold spices like ginger, cloves and cardamom. Sweet potato and butternut squash also roast beautifully into pies. Simply puree the flesh with non-dairy milk and spices.

Some festive plant-based pie combinations include:

- Apple - Apples, cinnamon, maple, vanilla
- Berry - Mixed berries, lemon, chia egg

- Pecan - Toasted pecans, maple, coconut sugar

- Pumpkin - Pumpkin puree, coconut milk, spices

- Key lime - Avocado, lime, coconut milk, graham cracker crust

- Chocolate - Silken tofu, cocoa powder, vegan chocolate chunks

- Banana cream - Bananas, vanilla, coconut whipped cream

- Strawberry rhubarb - Strawberries, rhubarb, orange zest

Making your own crust and fillings lets you control quality ingredients. But feel free to use store-bought components to simplify the process when needed.

Let cooled pies chill for several hours in the refrigerator to allow fillings to set before slicing. Garnish with whipped coconut cream, nuts or fresh fruit for added flair.

Homemade pies impress guests for special occasions. Swap in plant-based ingredients and no one will guess they're vegan. Fruit, nut and custard versions open endless possibilities beyond the traditional pumpkin and pecan. Bake a seasonal pie using fresh local produce. Slice up with love for a sweet treat any time of year.

Cakes

Baking a tender, frosted cake is a cherished tradition for many special occasions. Thankfully there are several easy substitutions that allow decadent cakes to be prepared without eggs, dairy or other animal products. With the right ingredients and techniques, vegan cakes can be just as indulgent. This chapter will explore how to adapt cake recipes, egg and dairy swaps, flavors, frostings and decorating ideas for sensational plant-based cakes.

Traditional cake recipes rely on eggs and butter for texture, structure and richness. To adapt for vegan diets, flax eggs, applesauce, aquafaba, bananas or silken tofu can provide similar binding and moisture. Oil, coconut cream, or vegan butter or margarine replace the dairy butter.

When using oil, decrease the other liquids slightly to avoid a too-wet batter. Vinegar or lemon juice help cakes rise. For fuller flavor, opt for oil blends like walnut or olive oil. The sugars and leaveners typically stay the same.

White, wheat, spelt and almond flours all work, or try a blend. Whole wheat pastry flour provides added nutrition without being too dense. Check labels on baking powder or soda to ensure no animal products.

Mix the batter thoroughly but gently to avoid toughness from over-mixing. Bake cakes at the temperature and time recommended, testing doneness with a toothpick. Allow cakes to cool completely before frosting for the best texture.

Explore flavors beyond classic vanilla and chocolate. Blend fruit purees or nut butters into batters. Citrus zests, coffee, spices, shredded coconut and espresso powder also infuse wonderful flavors.

Frost cakes with rich cashew or coconut cream-based frostings. Make a simple glaze by blending powdered sugar and non-dairy milk. Frost creatively with buttercream flowers, chocolate drizzle designs, shredded coconut or chopped nuts.

Here are some festive plant-based cake ideas:

- Classic Yellow Cake with chocolate avocado frosting
- Spiced Carrot Cake with vegan cream cheese frosting
- Strawberry Shortcake with fresh strawberries and whipped coconut cream
- Deep Chocolate Cake with chocolate ganache or raspberry drizzle glaze
- Pumpkin Spice Cake with maple cinnamon buttercream frosting
- Lemon Poppyseed Cake with lemon curd filling and glaze
- Tiramisu Cake with coffee syrup, cacao powder, and cashew mascarpone

- Tres Leches Cake soaked in 3 non-dairy milks
- Funfetti Cake with rainbow sprinkles mixed into vanilla batter and frosting

With some easy ingredient tweaks, both basic and elaborate cakes can be made vegan. Let your creative spirit run wild with unique flavor combinations, frostings and decorations. A sensational plant-based cake is sure make any celebration extra special.

Ice cream

Creamy, dreamy ice cream doesn't have to be off limits on a vegan diet. With plant milks, natural sweeteners and bold flavors, you can make homemade ice creams that rival the richness of traditional varieties. The base starts with blending up an ultra-smooth custard made from chilled non-dairy milk and starch.

For the milk, opt for unsweetened almond, soy, oat, cashew or coconut milk beverages. Full fat coconut milk adds luxe texture and tropical essence.experiment to see which you prefer. Avoid boxed plant milks as they can impart off-flavors.

Starch helps emulsify the milk to create a lush, creamy base. Tapioca, arrowroot or cornstarch dissolve smoothly when blended with chilled milk. 2-3 tablespoons thickens a standard batch.

Sweeten with unrefined natural sugars like maple, coconut sugar, agave or fruit juice concentrates. Dates or bananas also lend sweetness when blended in. Limit added sugars to let flavors shine. Stevia can help reduce glycemic impact.

Flavor with pure extracts like vanilla, almond, peppermint, coconut or fruit flavors. Try infusing milk with real fruits, herbs, spices or coffee. Cacao nibs or cocoa powder make chocolatey options.

Stir in any mix-ins after the base is chilled overnight. Nuts, chocolate chips, crushed cookies or candy integrate best when frozen into the solid base. Swirls of nut butter, jam or fruit puree create ripples of flavor.

Beyond classic vanilla, creative vegan ice cream ideas include:

- Chocolate Peanut Butter - use cacao and peanut butter
- Berry Swirl - raspberry/strawberry swirl
- Mocha Fudge - coffee infused with chocolate chunks
- Pumpkin Pie - pumpkin puree with cinnamon, ginger, nutmeg
- Chocolate Mint - mint extract and cacao nibs
- Cookie Dough - fold in vegan chocolate chip cookie dough
- Caramel Apple - caramel swirl with diced apples
- Coconut Lime - coconut milk with lime zest and shreds
- Blueberry Cobbler - blueberry swirl with oat crumble topping

For ultrasmooth texture without an ice cream maker, frequently stir the chilled base as it freezes every 30 mins until solid. Let soften briefly before serving.

Homemade plant-based ice cream lets you create fun flavors while controlling ingredients. With a simple base plus imaginative mixins, you can concoct creamy frozen treats without dairy or added junk. Sweet, chill and enjoy!

BONUS 1

AUDIOBOOK

Scan the QR code and listen to the audiobook in MP3 format

Harber Curry

BONUS 2

14 TUTORIALS FOR BEGINNERS

Scan the QR code and watch the video

Harber Curry

BONUS 3

47 ADVANCED TUTORIALS

Scan the QR code and watch the video

Harber Curry

BONUS 4

BASIC EVERYONE SHOULD KNOW

Scan the QR code and watch the video

Harber Curry

EXCLUSIVE BONUS

3 EBOOK

Scan the QR code or click the link and access the bonuses

http://subscribepage.io/01tYl3

AUTHOR BIO

Harber Curry

Harber Curry is a talented chef specializing in vegetarian cuisine, renowned for his skill in creating delicious and nutritious dishes. His passion for healthy and flavorful food has made him a prominent figure in the field of vegetarian cooking.

In addition to his culinary career, Harber is also a devoted husband and father to a beautiful family. His family is his inspiration and unwavering support, sharing precious moments together both at the table and in everyday life.

Harber has spent many years honing his culinary skills, studying vegetarian ingredients, and experimenting with new recipes. His dedication and constant pursuit of excellence have allowed him to create unique and highly regarded dishes enjoyed by his customers.

Beyond being a successful chef, Harber is a strong advocate for a healthy and sustainable lifestyle. Through his culinary talent, he seeks to raise awareness about the importance of a vegetarian diet for individual health and environmental sustainability. When he's not in the kitchen, Harber loves spending time with his family, sharing joyful moments and creating unforgettable memories. His passion for cooking is also reflected in their daily activities, where he engages his loved ones in exploring new flavors and preparing delicious meals.

Printed in Great Britain
by Amazon